My Book of Ruth

Reflections of a Jewish Girl

To Barbara & Jack,

Hoping to celebrate together
on August 28 in the future.

Zei gezunt

Ruth

My Book

of
Ruth

Reflections of a Jewish Girl

a memoir in thirty-six essays by
RUTH LEHRER

AUTHOR HOUSE

AuthorHouse™
1663 Liberty Drive
Bloomington, IN 47403
www.authorhouse.com
Phone: 1-800-839-8640

First published by AuthorHouse 1/5/2010

ISBN: 978-1-4389-7263-3 (hc)
ISBN: 978-1-4389-7264-0 (sc)

Library of Congress Control Number: 2009903812

Printed in the United States of America
Bloomington, Indiana

This book is printed on acid-free paper.

Cover Design, Title pages, and Contents pages
by Warren Lehrer

To Nathan and Simon

C O N T E N T S

Religion And Ritual

Retirement 1984

INTRODUCTION

Author's Note

I've written over a hundred personal essays in the past twenty years, but only a handful of them contain any Jewish content. My continuously evolving Jewish identity impacts so many areas of my life, yet I never felt the need to write about it. I don't choose my subject, it chooses me.

My two grandsons, *Bubeleh,* and his younger brother, *Shaineh Punim,* give me great joy and gild my "golden years." I give them my ear and they lend me theirs in return. When Jewish children reach the age of maturity (thirteen for boys, twelve for girls) they become responsible for their actions. A boy "becomes a bar mitzvah," a girl "becomes a bat mitzvah." When my older grandson turned thirteen, I wrote him a letter citing the grown-up characteristics he already possessed and describing my own coming of age more than six decades earlier.

For weeks after I sent that letter, I kept adding to it in my head. I wanted to broaden my grandchildren's awareness: of their secular grandma growing up in the Bronx, spending summers in a Catskill bungalow colony, her engagement with *Yiddishkeit;* their devoted grandpa, their immigrant great grandparents, my *zayde* (the family patriarch); religion and rituals, anti-Semitism, war and peace. It became an urgency I couldn't ignore.

Thus began "Reflections of a *Yiddishe Maidel,*" the essay. A Niagara of words poured out as I worked. My usual fifteen-hundred-word structure just couldn't cover everything I had to say on the subject. So I wrote another essay, then another, and another. For three years I quit my usual activities and holed myself up with my computer. Originally, I wrote with *Bubeleh* and *Shaineh Punim* in mind, but soon realized I was writing for myself. In pressing my nose against the looking-glass of my being, I had produced a volume-sized contemplation of my life as a Jewish American woman—*My Book of Ruth*.

A memoir in thirty-six essays—it is a montage of family portraits, history, religion, politics, philosophy, opinion, and Jewish cultural activity. Because the essays are thematic rather than chronological, they shift back and forth in time and between categories. Written the way I speak, they are sprinkled with Yiddish words, using the transliterated spellings I found easiest to read.

At my side in each piece, the other half of the "we" and the "us," is Arthur, Ma's *Favorite-Son-in-Law,* my high school sweetheart. Featured characters include *My-Son-*

the-Journalist and *My-Son-the-Artist*. Not until I completed rereading and editing all these essays, did I fully recognize the imprint of my *Yiddishe Mama*.

An immigrant woman with little formal education, Ma had a passion for the "Bintel Brief," an advice column in the *Jewish Daily Forward*, and for *The Goldbergs*, a sitcom radio program. Both venues were community and family oriented, just like my mother. I was surprised to find myself bumping into her in almost every corner I turned, a greater influence on me than any of the more worldly heroines I write about here. The seeds she planted are firmly rooted. I'm Ma's daughter, a *Yiddishe maidel*, following in her footsteps.

I considered using *Ma's Daughter* as the title for this book, but it didn't tell the whole story. *My Book of Ruth: Reflections of a Jewish Girl* — that seemed to say it all. *Girl* may sound politically incorrect and numerically inaccurate for an octogenarian's memoir, but I was a young girl when my chronicle begins, and that girl lives within me still.

1

Who Am I?

In 1952, just two hours after the birth of my first son, the cheery Italian woman in the bed next to mine was visited by a tall, dark, and very handsome young priest. *Is this hunk going to be celibate all his life?* I thought. After ten minutes with my roommate, he turned to me.

"I'm Jewish!" I cried out, fending him off with my out-stretched arm.

"That's okay," he said, "I'm just here to give you a bless-ing." Blessings by a rabbi had never been part of my life. Momentarily shaken, I quickly realized that this man in a white collar offered a prayer on my behalf, bringing with him the reality I still lacked: I'd be leaving this place with a real live baby, no longer a pretty, pampered, pregnant twenty-four-year-old, my life from this day forward forever altered. A blessing is a blessing, after all, and I needed all the help I could get.

Who am I? My first response, instinctively and without question, is "I'm Jewish"—mother, grandmother, American. What does it mean to be Jewish? It's a lifetime search. "You don't look Jewish," people have told me. I'm not too comfortable with that observation. Is it meant to be a compliment? On the other hand, I favor long skirts and long sleeves and have also been taken for Orthodox. I find that contradiction amusing. Heed the old adage not to judge a book by its cover.

The biblical Ruth (recognized as the first convert to Judaism) is considered an exemplary Jewess—which I am not. There are Jews today who may not even consider me Jewish. I might be deemed an *apikores*, a heretic. Am I a Conservative Jew? Reform? Reconstructionist? A Cultural, Humanistic, or Gastronomical Jew? None of the above. All of the above. There are lots of ways to be Jewish.

I dance the *hora* at weddings, eat Jewish food, and celebrate Jewish holidays—in my own way. I'm always on the lookout for books, plays, and film with Jewish content. Maintaining the principle of separation of church and state and preserving the Jewish tradition of social justice is high on my priority list. Zealotry, including Jewish zealotry, scares me. When I hear about a crime, I pray that the perpetrator is not Jewish. The Jewish Week is my preferred newspaper. My favorite place to browse is a Judaica gift shop.

The official name on my birth certificate is *Female* because my mother couldn't decide on an English translation for my Hebrew name, *Rivke*. That may be one of the few times in Ma's life when she couldn't make up her mind. It was many months, maybe even a year, before she settled upon *Ruth*. There were many of us Ruths born during the Depression era. I preferred *Rivke*, or the affectionate *Rivkele*, until at age nine, I discovered the *Book of Ruth*, a whole book in the Bible with my name. That's when I learned about Ruth and her special relationship with her mother-in-law, Naomi.

A dozen years later, on the first day of my first full-time teaching job in a Bronx elementary school, I met *my* Naomi. We were both clutching our appointment notices, both twenty-one years old, both idealistic and eager to embark on our chosen careers. Thus began a friendship that has existed for sixty years, and I expect it will endure for a lifetime. Our story is not parallel to that of the biblical Ruth and Naomi. Naomi is not my mother-in-law, and I am not a convert to Judaism. But the bond between us, the relationship of sisterhood and loyalty between women, portends a deeper meaning for me because of its association with the original Ruth and Naomi.

Strong, achieving women have made it to my list of heroines before the term "feminist" became a movement. I was about ten years old when Ma and I began listening to *The Goldbergs*, a radio show written by Gertrude Berg, who also performed the role of Molly, quintessential Jewish Mother and a bit of a *yenta*. Her fractured English made me laugh; the smile in her voice won my heart. Years later, I watched her on television, delighted to have found her again. I was in the audience when she starred in the award-winning Broadway show, *A Majority of One*, portraying a Jewish woman of a certain age involved in a romance with a Japanese widower. She won a Tony Award for her performance, but when the play was made into a movie, she was not chosen for the part. I wondered if she was considered "too Jewish." All the while, I saw Berg's career expand—in radio, television, film, and theatre, as performer, producer, and writer—a multi-talented woman in a man's world.

On an excursion to the 1939 World's Fair, I spotted Eleanor Roosevelt, first lady, walking along the promenade. She looked just like her picture in the newspaper, standing next to her husband, the president. For a few moments, I had the thrill of following her, but the tall woman in the rakish felt hat soon disappeared into the crowd. She didn't disappear from public life, however, and became known as "Eleanor Everywhere." I tracked her multi-faceted career— as journalist, United States delegate to the United Nations, chairperson of the Commission on Human Rights, and world traveler calling for nuclear disarmament—dedicated to promoting *diplomacy over force*. Ever since fourth grade, when I first learned that people killed one another in something called *war*, I've been distressed by mankind's inclination to use *force over diplomacy*.

I was a quiet kid. Teachers seemed not to notice me, which was okay; I liked it that way. Then along came Miss Robinson, my 200-pound fifth-grade teacher. One day she gave the class an assignment to convert Henry Wadsworth Longfellow's epic poem, *Evangeline*, into a play, to be presented at a school assembly program. It was a dream come true when she chose the one I wrote. My reward— getting to play the lead role—was more like a nightmare.

In class, I spoke only when spoken to. Speaking in front of a group was painful; performing on stage—even worse. My fantasies never included becoming Shirley Temple. But Miss Robinson persevered. Her guidance and encouragement got me through the performance—my first major triumph.

I was awed by these remarkable women—Berg, Roosevelt, Robinson—yet I believed that I would not, could not, follow in any of their footsteps. Growing up in a poor immigrant family, I was expected to graduate high school, get a job as a secretary, and contribute my salary to the family. Prepared to take some college courses at night, I was both astonished and grateful when Ma urged me to register as a full-time day student. It was Miss Robinson's caring image that guided me through student-teaching and my twenty-seven years as an elementary school teacher. Like her, I eventually settled into the fifth grade.

I adored the children, and treated them like my own. Some of them called me "Ma." I started each school year by giving a lesson on nutrition: dump the junk. After listing all the healthy (and delicious) snacks the kids could think of, I proposed using them at class parties. Parents were cooperative and innovative when planning their menus—peanut butter and apple slices, cheese cubes with carrot noses, fruit and nut mixtures, oatmeal cookies. (Only once did a parent balk.) The youngsters ate it up.

Teaching the kids to be *mentchlich* (good people) was my mission. Turning them on to the world of books was my most rewarding endeavor; correcting their written compositions, the hardest. Putting on original assembly programs gave me a high. (Miss Robinson, were you watching?)

In 1984 I retired from the classroom. Venturing into uncharted territory, I learned to square dance, joined a *Gurdjieff* study group, accepted a job as Elderhostel coordinator, traveled to warm climates in the wintertime, found Google. Most significantly, I followed my Muse, signing up for a course at the New School for Social Research—*Writing the Personal Essay.* No longer helping fifth-graders to write their stories, I began formulating my own. What an epiphany. By venting my emotions, I discovered the healing magic of writing! Since then, whenever I'm stressed, I sweep the monkey off my back and onto paper.

Most of my work deals with everyday concerns like family, friendship, natural healing, grandchildren, politics, and world affairs. In 1989, one year after I began writing, *The New York Times* published "Uprooting the Weeds of Winter's Discontent," the very first essay I ever submitted. *Hmm, this is easy,* I thought. Alas, I have yet to make it back into those pages. Some of my stories have found their way into anthologies for and about women: *Mother of the Groom, Women Celebrate, Chicken Soup for the Mom's Soul.* Some have appeared in Jewish magazines.

As I get older I become more aware of and concerned about worldwide issues. My viewpoints, filtered through Jewish sensibility, reflect the values I acquired growing up as a *Yiddishe Maidel.* Lawrence Bush, editor of *Jewish Currents,* echoes my thoughts when he writes: "There is a progressive pulse at the core of Jewish thought. It is this pulse—humanistic, engaged with the world, responsive to cultural evolution, dissatisfied with the status quo—that most keeps me engaged with Jewish identity and committed to its nurture."*

On the High Holidays my family gathers for a hearty meal, and we each consider possibilities for personal change and improvement. On Passover, we attend an extended family *seder*, eat matzah, and engage in a group reading from the Reform New Union Haggadah, depicting the biblical plagues in a contemporary light.

To remember upheaval that follows oppression, we pour ten drops of wine in hope and prayer that people will cast out the plagues that threaten everyone:
The making of war,
the teaching of hate and violence,
despoliation of the earth,
perversion of justice and government,
fomenting of vice and crime,
neglect of human needs,
oppression of nations and peoples,
corruption of culture,
subjugation of science, learning, and human discourse,
the erosion of freedoms.

The content of the prayer encompasses almost all of my major concerns. I am pleased that it assigns to us earthlings the responsibility for cleaning up the messes we make. Family members gaze at one another in meaningful silence before an impassioned discussion erupts. A new president has been elected and we hope to find ourselves back on the road to a kinder, more peaceful society.

* Lawrence Bush. "Judaism as a Counterculture," *Jewish Currents,* September-October, 2007.

IN THE BEGINNING

2

Coming To America

In 1910, Butche, my *zayde*, a thirty-nine-year-old *shtetl* Jew from Eastern Europe, decided to emigrate to America. A leather craftsman, who repaired shoes and created belts and bags in his shop outside Stanislaw, he could not eke out a living. Although Wechne, his wife, had inherited three small stone houses and Zayde's shop, as landlords they were poorer than their tenants and needed to beg for their rent money. I've been told that the weekly meat ration for their six children was the size of a quarter!

It was not just poverty that prompted Butche to leave his wife and children behind. Jews, over two million of them, from Russia, Poland, Austria, Hungary, Rumania, and Lithuania left for America between 1890 and 1914 because they were persecuted by governmental actions that made them third-class citizens. There were constant threats of violence. They were stoned and beaten, their houses burned. Strong, healthy, and hardworking, Butche would earn enough money to bring his family to America. And he would make it happen quickly. In New York they would have a better life.

Without her husband to help, Bubbe was having a hard time managing the property and feeding the children. As the eldest daughter, Clara (my mother), then twelve years old, took on most of the household chores. But it was still too much for Wechne to handle. To add to her woes, her two teen-age sons, Shmiel and Shlome, were constantly bickering with one another. Butche was no longer there to keep the peace between them, so Clara came to the rescue, devising a way to separate the two boys. She wrote her father a letter—and in 1912, Butche sent for Shlome. Now there were two family members in America, working to speed up the emigration process.

Father and son lived frugally. They rented space in a dormitory-style room on the Lower East Side, sleeping on bunk beds, along with a host of other immigrants. They put in long hours, working in a leather goods factory, then in a candy store, eventually selling fish from a pushcart. Finally, they accumulated the money they needed—but World War 1 intervened.

Russia was on the march. Shmiel was drafted into the Austro-Hungarian army, wounded, and sent back to the front. Wechne and her four youngest children were forced to evacuate their home. Along with their neighbors, they became refugees, and migrated to Czechoslovakia, where they remained for three years. While there, the entire family caught Typhus fever, a disease of the intestinal tract, rampant among soldiers from 1915-1918. Ruchel, Shmiel's robust fiancé, nursed them all. "They were good years," my mother told me. "The Czechs were kind, the best people we ever knew. The government gave us food and housing. We were no longer afraid."

They returned home to find their property destroyed by artillery barrage. Butche sent tickets for their second class passage to America, and the family took off for Paris, en-route to their ship in Le Havre. But once again fate intervened. Known as the "Spanish Flu" or "La Grippe," the influenza pandemic of 1918-1919 killed millions of people, more than were killed in WW1. In Paris, Ethel, the beautiful middle sister, caught the dread disease and was hospitalized for many months. The family crowded into a rented room, visited her daily, and waited for her recovery. When she was finally discharged, diagnosed with "sleeping sickness," she appeared to be in a semi-catatonic state. Everyone was heartsick; she was no longer the vivacious beauty they knew. And never would be again.

By that time their ship had already sailed, and in the process of exchanging tickets for a later date, dishonest shipping officials switched their second class accommodations to steerage, also known as third class, the lowest deck. The family was aware of unsanitary conditions down in the bottom of the ship—bad ventilation and filthy water closets. But immigrants were easy targets, and there was nothing the despondent group could do about it.

It was worse than they expected. Hundreds of people were herded together in one dark room reeking with the stench of vomit, eating on grimy benches along the sides of their small double-tier berths. But their biggest concern was Ethel: would she pass inspection at Ellis Island? Second class passengers were cleared on board by immigration officials upon arrival in New York. Steerage passengers were directed onto a ferry to Ellis Island where they had to pass a strict physical examination. Would they be sent back?

Like most of their fellow-passengers, the family fared poorly during the voyage, but managed to get through the examinations at Ellis Island. Surprisingly, so did Ethel, whose still beautiful young face and frozen smile fooled the doctors. It was Ruchel, having evaded Typhus Fever in Czechoslovakia, who contracted conjunctivitis in steerage, and was denied clearance! Shmiel declared he would not leave his beloved, and stayed on in Ellis Island until her discharge.

Instead of strong, handsome Butche dashing in to meet his wife and children upon arrival, it was Shlome who came; Butche had been stricken with a mysterious ailment, and was unable to walk. I can imagine how Wechne must have felt, so exhausted and frail was she from the voyage and the long difficult years away from her husband. Shlome was married now, and had rented an apartment for them on the Lower East Side. There they were, my *bubbe* and *zayde*, finally together again, with five of their children and a pink-eyed fiancé under one roof—a bittersweet reunion.

It was 1920, ten long years since Butche had left home! It was also the year that Congress passed laws severely restricting immigration, diminishing the flow of Jewish immigrants from Eastern Europe. Ruchel's family had intended to follow her, but unable to get into this country, they subsequently emigrated to Buenos Aires. After eight years of courtship, Ruchel finally married Shmiel, without her parents or sisters in attendance at her wedding.

Apprenticed to a watchmaker in Europe before the war, the groom had no difficulty finding a job. He taught Benny his trade and helped Clara get a job sorting watch parts. Ethel never recovered, and was institutionalized before her twenty-fifth birthday. Ceil went on to high school, the only one of Zayde's children to do so. In 1925, Shlome opened a fish store in the Bronx and moved the family up to Kelly Street, where Sholem Aleichem, the famous Yiddish storyteller, dubbed the Jewish Mark Twain, was known to have lived ten years before. Seven years after she arrived in America, Clara married Sam, a dry goods peddler. Ten months later I was born.

3

In My Jewish Home

My parents, both *greeneh* (greenhorns) from Poland, met on a blind date in 1927. Within the year they were married and living on Kelly Street, just one block from Bubbe and Zayde. Pa gave up peddling shoelaces and thimbles to sell porgies and smelts in his new brother-in-law's fish market on Jennings Street. Ma quit sorting jewelry parts when she became pregnant a month later. They spoke a combination of night-school English and *Galitziana* Yiddish in their strictly kosher home.

On Fridays Ma cooked and baked, then scrubbed the floors, covered them with old copies of the *Forvets*, and tore off sheets of toilet tissue in preparation for *Shabbes*. On that day we could not turn on the gas jets, use electrical appliances, write a letter, or ride the subway. My father spent the day in *shul*. Sometimes he took my young brother with him.

I wasn't expected to join them, except on *Simchas Torah*, the last celebration of the High Holidays. That's when all the children, girls as well as boys, crowded into the one room synagogue, carrying blue and white paper flags with apples skewered into the tops. We sucked on hard candy, we sang, we danced. It was the most joyous day in the year.

When I was in fourth grade, my parents enrolled me in Spectors' Talmud Torah. For four years, I spent weekday afternoons reading bible stories, studying Jewish history, and learning to read both Hebrew and Yiddish. I already spoke Yiddish fluently, so learning to read and write the language was like a puff of air. My mother read the "*Bintel Brief*" in her Yiddish newspaper each day, and I picked up her habit.

There was nothing religious or spiritual about my Jewish education. I don't recall our teachers making any references to God, although the references were there in abundance when we read the Hebrew prayers. Since Hebrew was not taught as a living language, none of us knew what we were reading or reciting. In those days girls did not receive Bat Mitzvah instruction. I'd rebel against it now, but at the time I just accepted the fact. A Bar Mitzvah was a boy thing.

Mrs. Spector distributed *pishkes* (collection cans) imprinted with the Star of David, and I'd go from door to door soliciting money for Palestine. Ma called it *Eretz Yisroel*. A decade later the United Nations carved out the tiny state of *Israel* from the British mandate for Palestine and created a Jewish homeland. When I was a youngster, collecting nickels and dimes for Palestine, I was under the impression that we already had a Jewish homeland.

Sunday was family day. Most of the time Ma's relatives would drop by in the afternoon. I'm sure her *ruggelech* laced with nuts and raisins were a major incentive. Occasionally we would take the subway "downtown" to visit my father's *mishpocheh* (family) on the Lower East Side. I didn't like their dark railroad flat and communal toilet in the hallway, and wondered why they lived there.

One Sunday a month we dressed up and went to *Bohorodzaner* Society meetings in Ratner's dairy restaurant on Delancey Street to meet with the *Landsleit* from my grandparents' hometown. Hundreds of thousands of foreign-born Jews belonged to *Landsmanshaften*, mutual benefit societies, composed of people who had come from the same community in the Old Country. At *Landsleit* meetings they talked about family left behind, life in America, and the workplace. They organized committees to call on the sick, to loan money, and to bury the dead. It seemed to me that everyone I met was some kind of cousin. A copy of a family tree would have been helpful.

I fondly recall a Society fundraiser called a "package party." Each family contributed a wrapped gift, which was then auctioned off, its content a mystery to the bidder. Ma took me with her to shop for something useful to bring. She didn't object when I chose a decorative, hand painted, carved wooden plaque. How wonderful it would have looked on our bare walls; I wanted to keep it for my very own. When our package came up for auction, my hand flew up and I bid twice what we paid for it. I looked at my mother, expecting her to be angry, but instead she patted my head. "It's okay," she said, "it's a donation." I don't remember where she hung it, or if she ever did.

Sometimes, Ma and I, dressed in our *Shabbes* clothing, would go to see a Yiddish play. We'd take a bus to McKinley Square theatre in the Bronx, or the subway to one of the theatres on Second Avenue in Manhattan. Movies were great, but live people on stage—singing, dancing, and emoting—were even greater. Light musical comedy, or serious drama (portraying and satirizing the lives of new immigrants), it didn't matter to me. I fully understood the language, although at age nine or ten, I may not have comprehended the deeper meaning of the melodramas I witnessed. Those were the most wonderful Sundays of all.

On Jewish holidays I helped my mother spread our pale green sateen tablecloth and set out the company china, wine glasses, and sterling silver candlesticks. I watched her prepare the familiar gastronomical *maykhels* (specialties)—*gefilte fish, lukshen kugel, gedempte flaish, tsimmis, strudel,* and *lakech.* How I loved a *puchke knaidel* in my chicken soup. For Yom Kippur dairy break fasts, I helped roll flour into dough for *pirogen, blintzes, ruggelach,* and *mandel broit.* On Pesach my father read the *Haggadah* from cover to cover for endless hours. I didn't mind. The *mishpocheh* was assembled and the special aura of holiday hung over our table.

President Roosevelt was not invited to our holiday dinners, but he was an honorary member of the family. We gathered around the radio for his *Fireside Chats,* an event equal in importance to our family gatherings. All the Jews we knew adored the president. He was my father's idol, "A fine man who inherited a Depression and created a *New Deal*." Pa championed everything the president accomplished—the WPA, the Social Security Act, the National Labor Relations Act. Imagine, giving workers the right to organize unions and to take part in strikes! He invoked Roosevelt's name in every sentence he spoke. "I think he's Jewish," he once told me.

The four of us lived in a one-bedroom apartment, and when my *zayde* moved in, there were five. It was crowded, yet spartan. There were no rugs on the floor, no Depression glass on the server, and nothing hanging on our cream-colored walls. The only non-utilitarian objects to be seen were an assortment of *pishkes* on the kitchen counter. My father never earned more than thirty-five dollars a week, but almost daily, I saw my parents feed a handful of coins into those collection cans. Designated for *Eretz Yisroel*, children's orphanages and yeshivas, the *pishkes* would then be picked up by black-garbed men with long white beards. I was accustomed to these strange looking people coming and going. And of course, like the building superintendent, the insurance agent, or anyone else who came to our apartment, they walked away with a bag full of home-baked sponge cake or *mandel broit*.

Years later, as teacher-advisor to the Student Union, I used the money we raised (at book fairs, bake sales, and bazaars) for charitable purposes. The class representatives and I prepared a list of environmental, health, and children's organizations, and the students voted for those they thought most deserving. When a new school principal arrived one year, he questioned my use of those funds and requested that I spend the money on school supplies. What supplies? There was no shortage of books or equipment in our school, and when I objected, he replaced me with another teacher. My fishmonger father would have made a better role model for our students.

Illness forced Pa to retire when he was fifty-seven, and he became part of a daily *minyan* (ten men gathered in prayer), his primary activity for the next twenty-five years. Yet, except for Shabbes restrictions when I was a child, and occasional expressions like *Gottenyu* and *Got-in-himmel,* he rarely invoked the name of God. A supernatural deity had not been part of everyday life in our household. Instead, I learned that being Jewish means you support unions, you favor equal justice for all, and you bring chicken soup to sick friends and relatives. Family is primary. You get together at Jewish holidays, and you take your children to the theater on weekends.

4

My Yiddishe Mama

Ma was a big woman. She may have measured only four foot eight, but she was a major presence in the life of those around her. Always in motion, I could never figure out why she wasn't skinny. She prepared healthy meals, served them, and did the dishes, but she never joined us at the kitchen table. I never saw her eat, and assumed it was the coffee she drank all day, with a half glass of boiled milk added to it, that kept her weight on. I couldn't look at that murky brown liquid. In my entire life I've never brewed myself a cup. If you come to visit, expect a *glazele* (glass) tea.

Growing up I thought of my mother as the typical *Yiddishe* Mama, a hard-working *balebuste* (housewife). She cooked, she baked, she kept our small apartment antiseptically clean. My two middy blouses were washed, blued, starched and ironed; my white shoes glistened. Always ready to be helpful, she scrubbed long underwear and graying curtains for my *bubbe* and *zayde* on her metal corrugated washboard. The forerunner of Fresh Direct, she delivered meals to her fragile sister, her ailing parents, her widowed cousin, a neighbor in need. Slowly, over the years, I came to realize that Ma was not typical at all.

Mrs. Berg sometimes helped her husband in their kosher delicatessen store in Harlem, and Ma offered to take care of their daughter, Harriet. People saw my mother shlepping both of us toddlers around. "Why are you doing this?" they asked. "Your husband earns a living." (A working mother was not common in the 1930s.) What she didn't tell them was that Harriet, the only other little girl in our apartment building, then became my instant playmate. Seeing her daughter playing happily was the only payment Ma wanted. A corned beef sandwich once in a while, with mustard and cole slaw, from Mrs. Berg's deli, was an unexpected bonus.

Life was *shver* (a trial), what with one thing after another to worry about. Ma wanted me to be happy, but not too happy. Who knows what will happen tomorrow? She warned me about the hazards of icy streets, traffic, and bicycle riding. If she saw a dog approaching, she gripped my hand and steered me in a different direction. She plied me with health food like Popeye's spinach and Squibbs cod liver oil. My winter coat pockets were stuffed with scarves and mittens. Accidents and illness were high on her worry list.

I have never forgotten that cold day in January when I was in first grade. I was dressing to go to a classmate's birthday party; it may have been my first, and I was so excited. Ma insisted that I wear leggings over long lisle stockings, and I refused. "All the other girls will be wearing anklets, and I'll be the only one with these ugly heavy things on my legs," I pleaded. "*Okshen*," she called me. She was only half-right. We were both *okshen* (stubborn). Neither of us relented, and I cried myself to sleep that night.

A few months later I caught a really bad case of the measles. Doctor Levinson came to see me almost every day. (Alas, doctors don't make house calls any more.) Through a haze I saw my mother hovering about my bed, not praying, but wringing her hands and pacing back and forth. It seemed to me that she thought I was dying, and I was scared. It must have been her spinach and cod liver oil that pulled me through.

The Bronx could be a cold nasty place in wintertime. Threatening weather forecasts were not issued from the radio every ten minutes in those days. If they were, no one in my family ever listened to them. Sitting in my junior high school classroom, seven long blocks from home, I'd gaze out the window at the unanticipated thickening clouds, the torrential downpour, the accumulating pileup of snow. Not to worry. I knew my mother would be at the exit door, SUPERMOM, ready to protect me from the elements. Gratefully I accepted her offerings—umbrella, raincoat, galoshes, boots, kerchief, sweater. I was only thirteen years old, and had become overcautious, just like her.

On *Shabbes* I watched my mother transform from a cooking, baking, and cleaning drudge into a fairy princess. The food we ate had been prepared the day before, and suddenly it seemed like there was nothing for her to do. She shed her flowered housedress and apron, and exchanged it for her *Shabbes* finery—a crepe, silk, or even satin frock. Gone were her matronly black or brown oxfords, and in their place patent leather pumps with Cuban heels (white in summers). Her dark hair shone, her strand of pearls and her one pair of earrings were in place. She read the *Forvets* and went out for a walk. I still picture her that way.

Ma had a cynical view of the rapidly changing society of the twentieth century—a world in which a *naya style* (a new style) confronted her each day. Take-out dinners? House-fathers? Nursing homes? "Women aren't women, men aren't men, family isn't family," she commented repeatedly as the years went by, shaking her head and mumbling to herself. "*A naya style.*"

"Today, friends are people you go to the theatre with, or out to dinner with—*a naya style.*" Friends were people she helped, the reason for being. If, on her birthday, I'd suggest going out for dinner, she'd refuse. "Go out? Why? Why should I eat out? I have a banana, some yogurt in the refrigerator, a can of salmon on my shelf. What do you eat in restaurants that you can't eat at home? Is it clean there? Do you know what they put in your food? *A naya style.*"

My mother joyfully dropped her maiden name when she married and became Mrs. Waldman. Best friends addressed one another by their new names—Mrs. Zeiderer, Mrs. Berg, Mrs. Fehrer. Young women, like her granddaughters, retaining their surnames after marriage? "*A naya style!*" When she moved into a senior residence in 1981 Ma became "Clara." She adjusted to this style, called her new friends Molly and

Rose and Lily. But when Clara became known as *PeeWee*, a nickname affectionately given her by a six foot, 250 pound male resident, she rebelled. Raising herself up to the full extent of her fifty-six inches she proclaimed, "Enough! I'm not PeeWee. I'm Mrs. Waldman. That's my name, again, and forever." It was *a naya style* she would not tolerate.

If life was a trial, Ma was the prevailing judge and jury. All my actions came under her jurisdiction. She always knew the "best" course of action, the "right" way to do things, and she managed to instill in me classic Jewish guilt. I became a perfectionist, always aiming to please her—and myself, always doing the best, the right thing. She never relinquished this role until her last years, when she was no longer in charge of my life—or her own.

I aimed to be a different kind of mother. I played with my children. I laughed with them. I didn't want them to become worriers. I think I succeeded. To this day they drop the monkey onto my shoulders, and I do all the worrying for them. My mother said whatever she thought—"whatever was in her head was on her tongue." Me? I walk on eggshells, monitoring my thoughts and my words, fearful of antagonizing my sons—or their wives. But if you ask them to describe their mother, I think they would be describing mine.

5

Sammy

Sam worked in Uncle Ben's fish market. He left early each morning, came home late each evening. He ate dinner alone, read the newspaper, listened to newscasts on the radio, and went to sleep. I heard his quiet whisperings with my mother from time to time, but mostly he was silent. When he spoke, he spoke to the walls, proclaiming his love of America, his indignation over injustices around the world, his horror of war. He never spoke directly to me. Indeed, my relationship with my father could be termed a non-event.

Did Pa ever hold me, feed me, wheel me in my baby carriage? I don't think so. Sam had a mission: to hand over his Friday paycheck, however meager, to my mother. He wanted nothing for himself. In doing this he was fulfilling his obligation as a husband—and as a father.

TV was non-existent in the 1930s and 1940s. *Father Knows Best* had not yet established Robert Young as a role model. I thought all fathers were distant shadowy figures, until I began visiting my friends. There I witnessed one father tousling his daughter's hair, another, asking questions about her homework and her teacher. These daughters were called "Honeybunch," or "Sweetiepie." Occasionally my father would call out to me, "Put on your galoshes," or "It's icy, stay home." I resented those warnings, did not recognize their caring.

How disappointed I was with him for not asserting himself with my mother. When I asked him a question, he inevitably replied, "Ask Mama." But Mama said "No" to all vital issues. He allowed her to make decisions I thought were unfair. He spoke out against oppressors all over the world. Why didn't he come to my defense?

I was a good girl. I always did the right thing. Yet, he never hugged me, or kissed me. I watched him with my brother. They talked, they played cards, had their heads together at the radio, and walked to *shul*, side-by-side. My brother was mischievous and got into fights; once the school principal sent for my parents. Still I saw his relationship with my brother prosper. How did that happen?

It is likely that my father was afraid of me, "Miss Perfect." He was orphaned at birth and raised by a classic "wicked stepmother" in an environment of pogroms and poverty. After World War I, his two older sisters, living on the Lower East Side, sent for him—a frightened, myopic, and under-nourished young man of nineteen. His biggest stroke of luck, he maintained, was meeting my mother. She fattened him up, got him a job, chose his clothes, made his decisions. He was safe. I think he could handle only one awesome female in his life. Had the principal called him to school on my behalf, if he had somehow seen me as flawed, perhaps he might have communicated with me more easily.

In fourth grade, I was absent from school for a few days, probably with a cold. Upon my return, I failed a history test I hadn't known about. That was a first for me. I never failed tests—not because I was so smart, but because I always did my homework and I always studied for tests. The teacher demanded a parent's signature and I was terrified. There was no way I could go to my mother. My father? Well, he was my only choice. When Ma was out of the house, I folded my test paper so that only some blank space was visible, and asked for his autograph. He looked at me quizzically, smiled, signed his name, and embellished it with ornate curlicues. Did he know I was putting one over on him? I never found out. The teacher had a signature, and I had a rare smile which I envision to this day.

I was twelve years old when my uncle asked me to help out in his fish market during the Easter/Passover holiday rush. There I saw my father, that quiet little man, hawking his wares at the outside counter, where the small fish were displayed.

"Porgies, smelts, shrimp, ten cents a pound," he shouted. "Come dahling, come sweetheart."

"Sammy," they bargained, "ten cents a pound?"

"For you, sweetheart, three pounds for a quarter, you can eat a whole week for a quarter."

They called him Sammy? Sammy was a pet name; my father was Sam, just plain Sam. From then on, I'd go to the store and hide in the shadows, just to watch him—a lamb turned into a tiger. He wasn't more of a father, but he was more of a man.

When he became a grandpa, my father seemed more comfortable in my presence. He spoke to my sons about war, and they heard him supporting every minority and underdog position the world over. He didn't exactly engage me in conversation, but he plied me with food—a bowl of my mother's split pea soup, a cup of tea, an apple.

At fifty-seven, chronically ill and legally blind, he retired from his counter in the fish market. When I visited him in the hospital, he could no longer avoid talking to me. Arthur helped him shave, and on my suggestion allowed a mustache to sprout. Voila! Plain little Sam, transformed into dashing Douglas Fairbanks. For a few weeks, before my mother made him shave it off, I basked in the aura of his new image—my father, the movie star.

My brother, Pa's confidante, died suddenly when he was thirty-nine, and Pa became more and more dependent on me. "Ruthie, what do you think, should I see another doctor?" "How do I protect myself against rent increases?" "Do I really need a new radio?" For the eight years preceding his death at age eighty-one, he wouldn't make a move without first consulting me.

My brother had been his friend; I achieved that status by default. We still didn't kiss or hug, but during those years when he seemed so vulnerable, my disappointment turned to compassion. Only then did I realize that he had been successful, fulfilling his goal in life, been a good husband, a good citizen, and what he considered to be a good father.

I picture Sammy in the kitchen of our Bronx apartment, his ear pressed against the radio speaker, sopping up the news, muttering aloud, and waving his fist. He may have been talking into the void, but it was his way of communicating with me all the while I was growing up.

6

Shtetl In The Bronx 1936-1948

Apartments were plentiful in the 1930s. Families moved frequently, from one building to another, to avoid the bother of painting and to get a month's concession. That was not my mother's style. For the first seven years of her marriage she lived in one apartment on Kelly Street, in the East Bronx, down the block from my *bubbe* and *zayde*—so she could "help out." Then, my only playmate, Harriet, moved out of the building. What's a mother to do? Ma, with a new infant to care for, moved the family out of Kelly Street to a dark, ground floor apartment "to-the-back"—ten long blocks away from her parents.

"To be near your cousins, so you'll have children to play with," my mother explained. Cousins Claire and Sara, both older, had their own friends. There were no other six-year-old girls in our building or on our block, so Ma's plan didn't work out too well.

Two years later, on a warm Sunday in June, we visited her cousins on Longfellow Avenue. Lo and behold, the street was alive with the sounds of children playing. Later that month, when the school term ended, we were living in a sunny apartment, one flight up and "to-the-front," on Ma's dream street, Longfellow Avenue.

Within the week Ma found a walk-in apartment for Bubbe and Zayde. From our bedroom window we could wave to them on their porch, directly across the street. Aunt Ceil and Uncle Reuben moved into the building next to us. Up the block lived cousins Harry and Esther, whose son was in third grade, just like me. Esther's sister Clara and her husband Sol lived down the street; their sister Pauline and brother Louis lived two streets down. Cousin Meyer, whose wife Yetta died from TB, and cousin Sura Hensha from Wilkes Barre, Pennsylvania, moved into the neighborhood in the coming years, completing our family enclave within our "shtetl" in the Bronx.

Never again did my mother need to worry about providing with me with playmates. The avenue was overflowing with boys playing stickball, Ringoleevio, and Johnny-on-the-Pony. Girls jumped rope (sometimes Double Dutch), skated, played jacks, and Pick-up Sticks. No play-dates for us. In the inimitable way of children, without introductions, former contact, or conversation, we just drifted toward one another and joined the action.

On my very first day in our new apartment, walking down the steep stoop of my building (which served as a community meeting area), I came upon some girls playing with pads of paper and sheets of colored pictures they called cocka-mamies, known as decals in modern jargon. For two cents I could buy these items in a candy store on Vyse Avenue, a few blocks away. So, clutching the pennies Ma happily gave me, I walked to the corner, up the hill and one street over, made my purchase, and started home. Suddenly, I found myself on a busy shopping street with lots of *gltizy* stores, and knew I had taken a wrong turn.

I don't remember if the policeman spotted me, or if I noticed him first, but there he was, at my side, a comfort-ing figure. How could he help me? He couldn't. I didn't know my house number, only that I lived on Longfellow Avenue. My mother, a chronic worrier, had not been con-cerned when I told her I was venturing off the street. The Lindbergh kidnapping notwithstanding, no one was going to kidnap a poor Jewish eight-year-old from the Bronx.

From the throngs of people passing by, a woman with frizzy gray hair appeared, told the policeman she knew my family and the apartment building I lived in, and volun-teered to take me home. The policeman handed me over, no questions asked. I'd never been warned about taking off with strangers, and I was grateful to be recognized. The woman took my hand and delivered me to my front door, to the girls who were still tearing and pasting their cocka-mamies. I never found out who she was.

My own, totally unofficial boundaries for our *"shtetl"* in the Bronx was Jennings Street to the south, Crotona Park to the west, Bronx Park to the north, and Boone Avenue to the east. My uncle's fish market, where Pa worked, was located on Jennings Street, the throbbing Jewish market-place, where you could buy a *tallis* for the Bar Mitzvah boy, a *reeb-izen* for grating potatoes, a *naya klaidl* (new dress) for the holidays. It was busiest on Thursdays, when people did their shopping for *Shabbes*. For Jewish holidays the women marched to the back of Uncle Benny's store, where they examined the large fish tank. The live whitefish and carp they selected for making *gefilte fish* sometimes ended up swimming in their bathtubs. Across the street was Hymie's famous pickle stand. Hymie gained notoriety for refusing to sell to people he didn't like. I knew I had passed his test when he plucked me off the end of the line and gave me a sour pickle—for free.

Crotona Park was where Uncle Reuben taught me to ride a bicycle. Sometimes he took me rowing on Indian Lake, which I quickly adopted as my own. On *Shabbes* I'd go for a walk around it. In winter I'd ice-skate on it. On Rosh Hashanah I cast my sins into it. What sins? I wondered, as I threw bits of bread into the water. I honored my parents, didn't steal, or kill anyone. Not for years did I consider the sins of jealousy, selfishness, intolerance, or impatience with my little brother. I don't think I ever took him to my lake.

As teenagers, we hung out in groups, marching off together to Bronx Park, exploring its lush grounds, larger and more exotic than nearby Crotona Park. None of us ever ventured onto Boone Avenue, just one block to the east of Longfellow Avenue, a dark, gray street of factories and other commercial enterprises.

Very few people on our street owned automobiles from the time we moved there in 1936 until I moved out in 1948, yet it was heavily trafficked. Horse drawn wagons came daily with fresh fruits and vegetables—*zup'ngreens* for chicken soup, cabbage for stuffing, onions for sauté-ing. Vendors pushed little carts selling jellied apples and apricots, wedges of coconut, and well baked sweet potatoes. Bungalow Bar and Good Humor trucks competed for our ice-cream sandwich, popsicle, and Dixie cup business.

The street functioned as the neighborhood Community Center, where all kinds of games were visible. My game of preference was marbles, *immies* we called them. They turned out to be my first exposure to the lure of gambling. I even became an entrepreneur. For one penny I purchased six marbles, and instead of patronizing one of the marble games lined up along the curb, I cut little doorways out of a shoebox and set up my own business. Gambling that their marbles would roll directly into one of those little door-ways, children ventured into the world of beating the odds. But just like in Las Vegas, they couldn't beat *the house*; I never lost my marbles. I accumulated nearly a thousand of them—from sky blue to ruby red, multi-colored, marble-ized and mottled, *realies, clearies, steelies*—the most success-ful, and only, business venture of my life.

The big social event for the kids in our building was Halloween. My parents thought it was an American holi-day. We weren't eating apple pie, but we were bobbing for apples. Originally a Celtic festival celebrated on October 31, the eve of All Saints'day, it is associated with ghosts, witches, hobgoblins, fairies, and demons. Children going from house to house demanding "trick or treat" and collecting money for UNICEF had not yet become the custom. We planned gala parties: decorations, food, games, scary stories. Almost twelve years old, and becoming aware of the opposite sex, I had been invited to my first, really big co-ed shindig. Thrilled to be included, I joined a planning session, paid my contribution, and spent a year's allowance on a señorita costume. But I was troubled. Two of my friends had not been invited, and they expected me to go to their party. What to do? It was probably the first major ethical decision of my life, and I was torn. Deep down, I think I always knew what I would eventually do.

On the big night, in my black patent leather sombrero with orange tassels, I ate candy corn and told ghost stories in a dark room, lit only with a candle inside a hollowed-out pumpkin, carved to resemble a demonic face. Sitting around the table, listening to the sounds of merriment on the fifth floor wafting down to our party on the fourth floor, were three young girls bravely trying to remain cheerful. In future years I was to be confronted with similar situations many times over, always needing to do the right thing, but not always happy when I did it.

Our building superintendent, Mr. Schmidt, one of the few non-Jewish people I encountered in the neighborhood, lived in a large ground floor apartment with a private outside entrance. He wore a suit and a tie, and knew how to fix everything. A stern authoritarian figure, he was the repository of building news. I considered him the president of our building. One day, hearing a hubbub in the hallway, I stuck my head out the door to find Mr. Schmidt revealing the shocking news that one of my friend's fathers had been shot, rumored to be part of a gang shooting. People stood there with their mouths open, shaking their heads.

A Jewish gangster? I couldn't believe it. To be Jewish meant to be honest, moral, and ethical. Weeks later, we learned that my friend's father was a labor organizer, gunned down for his union activities. That put a different light on the matter. Our neighbors were working people, my father an avowed labor advocate. Instead of a gangster, my friend's father turned into a martyr.

Not only were all the children in my apartment building Jewish, so were my classmates; my school could have been a *yeshiva*, but it wasn't. Classes gathered in the auditorium and teachers read to us from the *New Testament*. We drew Christmas scenes, sang *Silent Night*, and decorated Easter eggs. School was suspended for week-long Christmas and Easter vacations.

Not until I entered the "rapid advancement" classes in junior high school, to which children outside the neighborhood were admitted, did I come across kids who were not Jewish. Anthony was the handsomest, smartest, most personable boy in my class. Most of the girls had a crush on him. In 1941, in my *shtetl* in the Bronx, mixed dating was unheard of. I can imagine the grief it would have caused my family, had I brought home a non-Jewish boy. So imbued was I against the concept, I couldn't even allow myself the luxury of a crush on a Gentile boy.

At fifteen, going into the second half of my junior year at James Monroe High School, my friends and I joined Starlight, a neighborhood pool club for teenagers. Clusters of girls, in their one-piece bathing suits, hung out on the man-made sandy beach, while groups of boys with stylish pompadours looked to join them. It was a summer of many firsts—the first time my family didn't go to a Catskill bungalow colony, the first time I had a job other than babysitting, and the first time I jitterbugged with a "professional" dancer.

On weekend evenings live swing bands provided "dancing under the stars." Some of the young dancers I watched were awesome. The very best of them, I'll call him Fred, as in Astaire, was reputed to be "a professional dancer, a high school dropout, a drug user, and—probably not Jewish." When he asked me to dance I was flustered. *A high school dropout? Using drugs?* Worst of all, *not a Jew?* Forbidden fruit. Yet, I was flattered to be chosen.

He must have seen me dancing. I'd been jitterbugging and doing the Cha Cha, the Rhumba, and the Fox Trot since I was thirteen. Dancing was my blossoming passion. After our first dance, he asked for another, then another, all in silence. "*Sh*," he whispered, when I asked him a question, concentrating instead on twirling and dipping. For half an hour he made me feel like Ginger, but I was getting nervous, already picturing my mother's head in the oven. That's when I spotted Artie, one of the beach boys, a blonde kid with a wavy pompadour. I announced to Fred that my "date" for the evening had arrived, and made my getaway.

Who knows? Fred could have been an honor student at Yeshiva High School. But it was Artie who became my dancing partner for the rest of the summer. He looked like a young Harry James, my favorite band leader, and was going into his junior year at the Bronx High School of Science. I was impressed; that's where the brainy boys went. When school resumed in September, we were already "going steady," which for us, at fifteen-going-on-sixteen meant going to the RKO Chester every Saturday night and ordering black and white ice cream sodas after the movie.

We were married five years later, in the hottest wedding ceremony any of our guests can remember—98 degrees. (The following summer air conditioning hit the Bronx.) Artie's parents had relocated to California, and not yet twenty-one, the legal age for voting, boozing, and marrying, he needed their written permission. I had graduated from college the week before; my new husband, recently discharged from the army, had two years to go. We had no money, no jobs, and no place to live. Chutzpa? Stupidity? Hormones?

Apartments were scarce in 1948. Instead of concessions to renters, people offered money "under the table," if they were lucky enough to learn of a vacancy. So we rented a bed on the western rim of our *shtetl*, in an elderly widow's living room, which smelled of the rat poison she sprinkled on the baseboards. Three months later my best friend's father, a landlord, offered us a studio apartment with a sunken living room, in a building just off the Grand Concourse—no money under the table. How lucky can you get? And so I had the distinction of becoming the first member of the family to move out of our enclave on Longfellow Avenue. During the next ten years every one of us moved, not only from our *shtetl*, but from the Bronx.

7

People Like Us

I was ten years old in 1938. My friends were going off to the Y sleep-away camp and I told Ma I wanted to go with them.

"People like us don't go to camp," she declared.

"But Winnie is going, and so are The Twins," I protested.

"Their fathers are business people," she explained.

"Vera's father works for the post office."

"He'll have a pension."

"If we can't afford to pay, the lady at the Y said we won't have to."

"If we can't afford to pay, we stay home."

I never got to sleep-away camp—not that year, or any other.

"People like us don't go to camp." Those words rattled around in my head. There were so many things *people like us* didn't do.

My father sold fish in Uncle Benny's store. He earned just enough money to pay the rent for our three-room apartment and to buy food for the delicious meals my mother cooked up. I knew that beneath her stern exterior lay her fears: my mattress would be infected with fleas; I would drown in the lake; I'd be prey to bears and wolves, maybe even tigers. Worse yet, I would contract polio. Look what happened to Grandpa.

My *zayde*, a virile immigrant in New York, ready to conquer the world, had indeed succumbed to polio. Paralyzed and unable to walk, he came to live with us when I was fourteen. "Where will you put him?" everyone asked. Ma stretched the walls of our tiny apartment—created a dormitory in our one bedroom for him, my father, and my brother, while she and I became roommates in the living room. I watched her scrub her papa's soiled underwear, bring his favorite foods into the bedroom, and help him to the bathroom—the only walk he ever took. But she never complained. *People like us honored our mothers and our fathers.* I thought that's what all families did for each other.

People like us didn't go to camp. But did they play the piano? Seated around the table at a Passover *seder*, Uncle Benny announced that his neighbors were selling their old upright mahogany piano. I thought everyone in the room could hear my heart thumping. Would this be the answer to my not-so-secret dream, taking lessons and learning to play?

"Ma, please, can we buy that piano?" I pleaded.

"People like us don't buy pianos," she answered, not unexpectedly. Uncle Benny offered to pay half of the awesome price of fifty dollars. I glanced at Ma's expressionless face, daring to hope. Ma asked about piano lessons and music books. And where would she put a piano anyway? How far could walls stretch?

Ma was proud. *People like us* don't go to camp. *People like us* don't buy pianos. Yet, there were little collection cans strewn around the kitchen in which we deposited pennies, nickels, and dimes for the orphans, the sick, and the elderly. *People like us* gave to charity. We were not recipients.

I grew up knowing what *people like us* did and didn't do. I knew it was the family expectation that when I finished high school, I'd quit my part-time job as a stock clerk, become a secretary, and contribute my salary toward household expenses. That's what *people like us* did in the Bronx in 1945, when very few high school graduates went on to college. But as graduation day drew closer, and I saw some of my friends preparing to go to Hunter or to City, both tuition-free city universities, I dared to envision myself a co-ed, in saddle shoes and Chesterfield coat. Once again, I confronted my mother.

"Winnie and The Twins are going to City College," I began. "I want to go too. If I enroll as an evening student, I can work during the day and...." My mother, shaking her head, didn't let me finish. My stomach flip-flopped. I knew what was coming next.

"You know what will happen if you go to school at night for years and years, after working all day?" she asked. "You'll be worn out and discouraged. You'll never graduate and you'll be a drop-out." Then she added, "Go to college full-time, during the day, and continue working part-time."

"But, but," I sputtered, "what about my secretary's salary? I only earn fifty cents an hour working at Klein's."

"If you pay for your books, clothes, and carfare, we'll manage without your salary. And I'll pack you a lunch every day." I was overwhelmed. Imagine—*people like us going to college*—full-time, during the day!

Ma kept her part of the bargain. For four glorious years I avoided cafeteria burgers and fries, and shared my salmon croquettes and almond cookies with my House Plan sisters. There's a picture of us in my scrapbook. I'm the one in the middle—with saddle shoes and Chesterfield coat.

8

Get The Jews

How lucky my parents felt. As immigrants to the United States, "Get the Jews" was no longer the fear they lived with. They trembled when they heard about *Kristallnacht* in 1938, instigated by the Nazis all across Germany. But that was in Europe. They seemed not to be aware of anti-Semitism in this country. If they were, they didn't want to hear about it. This was their *Goldene Medina*.

But anti-Semitism was alive and well in the United States. In the south, white-robed Ku Klux Klan members boycotted Jewish merchants, vandalized their stores, and burned crosses outside synagogues and other Jewish in-stitutions. Henry Ford circulated the anti-Semitic forgery, "The Protocols of the Elders of Zion," in his newspaper, The Dearborn Independent. Father Charles E. Coughlin's hate broadcasts could be heard on the radio nationwide. German-American Bundists paraded swastikas and Nazi flags, mostly in New York. Every synagogue in Washington Heights was desecrated from 1942-1945. Job discrimination and educational quotas were tolerated. Only 10 percent of the Jews eligible to enter this country under established quotas were permitted to do so.

World War II—after living through the horrors of World War I, my parents couldn't believe it was happening again! Another war? In bits and pieces news about the Holocaust was coming out—ghettoes, concentration camps, and the systematic extermination of six million of our people. None of us knew that President Roosevelt, the man our family revered, had turned away a boatload of Jewish refugees seeking shelter, sending them back to certain death in Germany. "Political *chozzerai*," my father would have said. He wouldn't listen to any criticism of his president, or of his country.

My sweet sixteen year was not so sweet, mired in a period of family grief and mourning. My brilliant nearsighted cousin Abie was killed in the Battle of the Bulge, the bloodiest encounter the U.S. forces experienced in the war. He was eighteen years old, a senior in college, and my inspiration for going to college. Shortly afterward we learned that Grandpa Israel had been killed in the Holocaust. Was he thrown into a pit and shot? Herded into a gas chamber and gassed? Or shoved into an oven and incinerated? I'm glad I never knew. Killing one another as a means of problem solving was beyond my comprehension. It was something barbarians did a long time ago, not modern civilized people.

After the war, the victorious Allies founded the United Nations, a global organization that would protect peace, provide a forum for international discussion, and promote freedom around the world. I considered it a beacon of sanity and hope for the future. In 1947, recognizing the world's complicity in the most massive genocide ever known, the UN adopted Resolution 181, portioning off a sliver of land from the original Palestinian Mandate under Great Britain, to create a Jewish state. When Israel declared her independence in 1948, I was ecstatic—a Jewish homeland, acknowledged at last.

I was in college when the Anti-Defamation League (ADL) waged a campaign against discrimination in housing, employment, and education. By 1947, Federal law required employers to remove the question about *religion* from their employee application forms. But were they removing it? I volunteered to work with the ADL to test compliance with the law. My mission was to obtain job application forms for them to scrutinize. I would apply for a job as secretary, file clerk, or bookkeeper at a variety of business establishments suggested to me by the ADL, and instead of submitting the completed application form to the employer, I'd casually stuff the evidence into my purse and make my getaway— Nancy Drew, girl Jew, doing her part in the struggle for equality.

I graduated from college, got married, and started teaching in a Bronx elementary school. Arthur and I celebrated our first anniversary in a Catskill hotel. While there, in sailor suit or hula skirt, we joined the chorus of an amateur production of *South Pacific*. Its theme, you've got to be taught to hate, was without precedent for a big Broadway musical in the 1940s. I was haunted by the show and wrote a parody of it for my second graders' assembly presentation. The principal asked us to perform it for the entire school.

After World War II, Bess Meyerson was crowned Miss America, Milton Berle became the darling of Tuesday night television, and Hank Greenberg was admitted to the Baseball Hall of Fame. My sons were accepted into the Ivy League schools of their choice, and I was never asked to re veal my religious identity on a job application. The dream of equality and acceptance into American society appeared to have become a reality. Life was good for the Jews.

9

Zayde

Ma wheeled me along Kelly Street in my wicker stroller to where Bubbe and Zayde lived just two blocks away. Every morning she showed up to help with the laundry and the cooking, stopping off to pick up some sour cream, a fresh killed chicken, some *zup'ngreens*. Bubbe suffered with headaches, and I never saw her without a wet *shmatte* on her head. Nobody put a name to Zayde's useless legs, but the family surmised it was polio. For a few years he was driven to Uncle Shlome's fish market where he tended the cash register, but finding it increasingly difficult to get around, he reluctantly resigned himself to staying home.

My *zayde*, Butche, in his late fifties, round and cuddly, with a mustache and trim beard turning gray, sitting in his armchair next to the parlor window, couldn't wait for me to arrive. When I ran into the room and climbed onto his lap, a smile lit up his face and the years dropped away. He couldn't take me to the park or ride me on his back, but he'd tickle my palm, mumble something that sounded like *keezele myzele*, and make me laugh. Then, for the rest of the morning, as the aroma of Ma's chicken soup floated through the apartment, he would transport me to another world, conjuring up his famous *bubbe-meisehs*, one after another. "*Nuja Zayde*," I would nudge him when he stopped to catch his breath, and the next fantasy—about a foolish man, a poor orphan, a trickster, a fairy godmother perhaps—would come tumbling out of him. How lucky I was.

I was eight years old when my family moved to Longfellow Avenue; my grandparents followed soon afterward. I could see their apartment from our bedroom window. Poor Bubbe's headaches were getting worse and she was spending more and more time in bed. Those long hard years in the Old Country during the war, alone with five of her children, and Butche working across the ocean, were taking its toll. "Don't stay too long," Ma warned me when I crossed the street to see them. "Bubbe needs to rest." Sometimes my *bubbe* was up and around, and she'd give me one of Ma's *ruggelech*, and kiss me. On those days I saw her smile, her beautiful sweet smile. I'd watch Zayde follow her with his eyes, and he looked so sad.

I was a third-grader then, too big for Zayde's lap, and too old for his *bubbe-meisehs*. Instead, he taught me to play Casino, his favorite card game. I taught him to play War, but he wouldn't play a game with that name. "War is not a game," he scowled. He introduced me to Pisha Paysha, similar, but requiring more strategy.

Although I saw him using *tefillin* (ritual prayer objects), and he lived next door to the *shul*, Butche didn't make the effort to attend, not even on Yom Kippur. Maybe he didn't see a connection between going to synagogue and being a good Jew. Yet, I remember him donating a Torah to the synagogue. Who could forget? It was such a big deal. A throng of exuberant Jews paraded through the streets of the Bronx, behind Zayde in his rented wheel chair holding the *Sefer Torah,* then crowding into the tiny *shul.* I marched along with them, infected with their pride, and wondering where he got the money to obtain such a precious commodity. Years later I learned that someone had bequeathed the Torah to him, so that he could donate it and receive the honor.

Bubbe was becoming progressively frail, frightened, and forgetful, rarely coming out of her bedroom anymore. "Hardening of the arteries," they said. Alzheimer's, we call it today. In those years families suffered in silence, even shame. By the time I was fourteen, she required skilled nursing care, and could no longer remain at home. That's when Zayde moved in with us—more work for Ma—a treat for me.

Each day, after school, I carried a glass of milk, a *glazele* tea, and some butter cookies to where my *zayde* sat by the fire-escape window. He'd pull out the deck of cards he'd been shuffling for hours, and we'd play our usual Casino and Pisha Paysha. I'd learned to play Rummy by then, and we added that to our repertoire. We'd play and eat and drink and talk, and that's when Zayde became my best friend and confidante. If anything was troubling me—school, boy-friends, Ma's restrictions—I went directly to him for an *etza*, a solution to my problems.

People loved and respected this man. He was credited with bringing thirty-five family members to the United States. He didn't have any money, so I'm not quite sure how he did that. Most likely he sponsored them and vouched for their self-sufficiency. Everyone wanted his ear. *Mishpocheh* dropped in to talk to him at all times of the day. His son-in-law, my Uncle Reuben, appeared each morning before going to work, to help him get dressed and just to shmooze. On Fridays, Uncle Benny, his youngest son, arrived to bathe him and to discuss business. Relatives from as far away as Mexico and Argentina found their way to our apartment, seeking an *etza*.

Nine months after I was married, my *zayde* died in his sleep. He was seventy-seven years old. I was substitute teaching when I got the phone call, and too shaken to fin-ish my day's assignment. The following day, on the way to the funeral, I watched my cousin Estelle chatting away and laughing. *How can she be so casual? Doesn't she feel the pain I'm feeling?* At the time I didn't consider that I alone had spent time with him almost every day for the twenty-one years of my life. How could any of Zayde's thirteen other grandchildren have felt the way I did? Three years later I named my first son after him.

On the last day of *shivah* (mourning week), my friend Pearlie, a college House Plan sister, was getting married in the wedding gown I'd worn just nine months earlier. I knew it was inappropriate for a Jew in mourning to attend a *simcha* (celebration) where music was playing and people were dancing. Still, I was bereft at not being present for her wedding, as she had been for mine. What should I do? I could no longer go to my *zayde* for an *etza,* but I knew what he would say: *"Gai gezunterhait un farbrengzich gezunterhait."* (Go in good health and enjoy yourself in good health.) But how could I?

THE JEWISH AMERICAN EXPERIENCE

10

Yiddish, Yinglish, Oy Vey

For nearly a thousand years, Yiddish was the primary language that Ashkenazi Jews spoke. Beginning in the tenth century, Jews from France and Italy established large communities along the Rhine River in Germany, and spoke a modified version of medieval German. In the 13th century, Jews migrated eastward to escape persecution, and Yiddish went from a Germanic dialect to one that incorporated elements of Hebrew, Aramaic, Slavic and Romance languages.

In the 19th century, the language became a means of describing the vibrant life that had developed in the ghettos and *shtetls* of Eastern Europe. It spawned Yiddish authors like Mendele Mocher Sforim, Sholem Aleichem and Isaac Leib Peretz who are today considered important literary figures by non-Jewish and Jewish critics alike. At the height of its usage, Yiddish was spoken by millions of Jews of different nationalities all over the globe.*

David Shyovitz

Ma didn't waste much time after landing in America before enrolling in a night school class to learn English.

She spoke Yiddish to Bubbe and Zayde, and practiced her new language with her siblings, cousins, and co-workers. She had been in this country for eight years before I was born, and spoke to me using a *mishmash* of both Yiddish and English.

Every day, for the first five years of my life, we would visit my *bubbe* and *zayde*, who spoke no English. Like Sholem Aleichem, my *zayde* was a masterful storyteller, and he'd fill my head with fanciful tales, all in Yiddish. Each story began with *"A mol is geven"* (once upon a time), and most were inspired by the ethics and morals of the Torah:

It was a *shande* (shameful) to be: *foil* (lazy), *ongue blozen* (conceited), *chutzpadik* (brazen), *baiz* (angry), *narish* (foolish), *shmutsik* (dirty), *a shnorer* (a beggar), *a ligner* (a liar), *a shlechte mentsh* (a wicked person).

A *mentsh* (person of integrity) was: *a shver arbiter* (a hard worker), *pinktlich* (prompt), *erlich* and *emisdek* (honest and truthful), *guelerent* (learned), had *rachmones* (compassion), and did *mitzvahs* (good deeds).

Zayde's messages codified my behavior for the rest of my life.

I was three years old when Aunt Ceil, Ma's youngest sister, married Uncle Reuben, a "Yankee." On weekends they'd take me to their home for sleepovers; we spoke no Yiddish, only English. One could say I was *bi-yingual*. I would describe my language pattern as a *bissel farmisht* (a little mixed up).

When I was nine, my parents sent me to *cheder*, where along with Hebrew, I learned to read and to write the Yiddish I was already speaking. Pa read the *"Forvets"* (*Jewish Daily Forward*) from cover to cover, and I began reading Ma's favorite column, the "Bintel Brief." What an education I received. Forerunner to "Dear Abby," it doled out advice to its readers—to people who earned just pennies a day, people who worked in sweatshops, and to people whose jobs were at risk because they were *Shabbes* observers. Husbands left their wives, boarders had romances with the woman of the house, freethinkers were flaunting the mores of society. One man was afraid to marry his sweetheart because she had a dimple in her chin; he was told that the first spouse of a dimpled person dies at an early age! I was a kid, learning about the *tsuris* (troubles) that immigrants were experiencing in America. I consider the "Bintel Brief" a major contributor to shaping the social and political views I hold to this day.

By the time I graduated from grade school, English had become my parents' primary language. They still read the *Forvets*, but they believed we were an American family, and "Americans speak English." Zayde moved in with us when I entered high school, and he spoke to me in Yiddish. I responded in English or Yiddish. Either way, after forty years in this country, he understood me.

By the late 1940s, the Holocaust and the repression of Soviet Jews under Stalin resulted in the dramatic decline of Yiddish spoken world-wide. As the number of American born Jews increased, Yiddish also lost its status as the primary language of the American Jewish community. It surprises and saddens me when I come across Jews who are my contemporaries, and who don't understand or speak the language at all. Fortunately, Hassidic and Orthodox Jews continue to use Yiddish as their primary language, and it is now studied in non-Jewish and academic worlds.

Arthur and I met when we were in high school. As teenagers, we were about equal in our ability to speak Yiddish, but as second generation Americans, we rarely spoke it with one another. Over the years, however, we began injecting more and more Yiddish words and expressions into our conversation—*Yinglish,* I called it; I thought I had coined that word. But in *The Joys of Yiddish,* author Leo Rosten uses the word *Yinglish* to describe *new* words created by Yiddish/English speaking people, an altogether different meaning from mine.

There's a whole generation of us Jewish *kids*, born to immigrant parents in the 1920s and '30s, who speak English sprinkled with Yiddish, my form of *Yinglish*. This e-mail, sent to me by my cousin Judy, is an example—a slightly exaggerated spoof of the way we speak.

> "To all the *shlemiels, shlemazels, nebbishes, nudniks,* and *momzers* out there, I would like to say I get sentimental just thinking about English. When I listen to these *mavens* and *luftmentshen* who want to add Spanish to our national language, it makes me so *farklempt,* I'm fit to *plotz.* What *chutzpah!*"

About five hundred Yiddish words have been incorporated into the English spoken in the United States today—words like *nudnik, shalom, borsht, mazeltov, yenta, kibbitz, kvell, kvetch, mitzvah, nosh, nebbish, klutz, knish, schmaltzy,* and *zaftig.* Many Yiddish words lose their true meaning when translated into English.

Arthur tells a story about Izzy, who receives a painting from his wife as a twenty-fifth anniversary gift. He gapes, open-mouthed, at the all-white canvas with a single black dot on it—*Man Alone in the Universe.* He thinks it's a hoax, but over the years he develops a great fondness for it. For their fiftieth anniversary, his wife gives him another white painting, this time with two black dots on it—*Man Alone in the Universe with His Mate.* Izzy stares at it, and stares at it. "*Nu?*" his wife asks. "What do you think?" Izzy stares a little more. Finally he blurts out, "It's *ungepatchket.*"

I cannot ascribe a one-word English translation to this word. It could be a manner of dress or decorating that would be cluttered and clumsy, too loud or too colorful, with an assortment of plaids, stripes, and floral patterns, beads and bangles. It could be overdone, in bad taste, garish, and declassé. In Yiddish, it's *ungepatchket,* a fun word in a fun language.

What a mistake I made by not speaking this precious pearl of a language with my sons. These days even second and third generation immigrants to this country use their native tongue when communicating with each other and with their children. Speaking or listening to Yiddish makes me smile. I robbed my boys of this pleasure. There is no doubt in my mind that they would feel more connected to their Jewishness if they understood and spoke the language.

Arthur and I use Yiddish as code when we don't want people to understand what we're saying. I once found myself speaking the language when we were walking our friend's dog! We used Yiddish as code with our sons too, but they usually caught on. When they heard one of us say, "*Luz Em*" (let them), without knowing what it meant, they knew their request would be granted. "Ma, can we go to the Yankee game this weekend?" "*Luz em, luz em,*" they'd squeal, if they saw us deliberating.

After the boys were out of the house, their father and I tried to revive our Yiddish conversation, but it was rusty and halting. We went to a Yiddish *Vinkel* (club), but the members spoke quickly and read literary works that were beyond our comprehension. It's not like riding a bicycle; when you don't use it, you really lose it. Who better to practice with than Ma? But Ma had lost it too. She spoke mostly English and Leo Rosten's *Yinglish*, using *new* words created by Jewish speaking people.

"Ma, how would you say a *successful person* in Yiddish?" I asked.

"An *alrightnik*," she answered, shrugging her shoulders.

"What's the Yiddish word for window?"

"*Vinda*, what else?" A liar was a *bluffer*, someone she didn't like was a *no-goodnick* or a *shmegegge*. The person in the apartment below her was the *downstairseke*.

Ma spoke her *Yinglish*, and I speak mine. I do not refrain from doing so in conversation with my grandchildren. "*Bubeleh, Shaineh Punim,*" I call them, pinching their cheeks lovingly when we meet. *"G'valt!"* I groan, when I see them wearing nothing but tee shirts on a cold wintry day. We all laugh. They've picked up a few Yiddish words, but without continuity they remember *bubkes* (very little). Certainly they understand more than their father does.

"Zie Gezunt" (be healthy), the Chinese owner recently declared as our family was leaving his restaurant. *"Zie Gezunt,"* Arthur and I both replied.

"Why didn't you respond to him?" I asked my son when we were outside. "I don't understand Chinese," he said.

Oy Vey!

* David Shyovitz. "The History and Development of Yiddish," www.jewishvirtuallibrary.org, excerpts reprinted with permission of the author.

11

Jewish Women In The Catskills

SUMMER IN THE CATSKILLS, circa 1935. In a crowded bus, a hired hack, or Uncle Benny's new DeSoto, my family escaped from our hot apartment in the Bronx to the healing *luft* (air) of "The Mountains." We trekked up Old Route 17, stopping when any of us kids became carsick, or for lunch at the Red Apple Rest. For over seventy years, small *shtetl*-like villages in Sullivan and Ulster Counties such as Monticello, Loch Sheldrake, Ellenville, and Liberty were summer homes to Jewish vacationers.

Ma first sampled *a kokhaleyn* (American Yiddish word for a rooming house with communal cooking facilities) in Fleischmanns, high in the mountains, where she shared a huge kitchen with more than a dozen other women. "It wasn't easy, each of us scrambling for a gas burner or a place at the sink," she repeated over the years, "but the *luft* (air) was better up there. It was during the Depression, and inexpensive, maybe

$25 or $50 for the whole summer. After that, I found a small hotel in South Fallsburg, the same money for a two-week stay. We dressed up every night, our meals were served to us, it was luxury. But I wanted to get out of the city for the whole summer, so we ended up in a "bungalow colony."

Our small family, along with aunts, uncles, and dozens of cousins, spent eight glorious summers in one and two-bedroom white clapboard bungalows, set on a forest-rimmed clearing in Woodbourne, each with a large, screened-in porch. It was women and children only, those weekdays in the summer Catskills—except for my grandfather, afflicted with polio and confined to his armchair on the porch. Only during a weeklong vacation stay were husbands and fathers to be seen midweek on our campus.

I suspect it was not only the *luft* that brought the women to the mountains. They appeared to enjoy their brief escape from traditional housewife roles. They read, had intimate discussions, skinny-dipped in the Neversink River, and played cards. Rarely had I seen my mother laugh before, or with free time on her hands. Meals were simple: vegetarian dishes like noodles with cheese, and bowls of huckleberries with sour cream. Mothers and children went berry-picking most days and took long walks on country roads into the nearby villages to shop. Sometimes we even dared to hitchhike.

Yet my warmest memories center around preparing for the weekend: cleaning the bungalow, helping my mother shell peas and chop onions, washing my hair, and putting on my best clothes. It was Friday, and the Daddies were coming up from the city, bearing bialys, challah, and an assortment of *tchotchkes*. The aroma of *mandel* bread and blueberry pies baking in the oven filled the air. The early 1940s were much the same, overshadowed by the absence of our male cousins gone off to war and the emerging news about family left behind in Russia and Poland slowly entering our consciousness.

I never saw the elegant, resort side of the Catskills—the Nevele, the Concord, Grossingers, Kutshers or Brown's, with their indoor-outdoor swimming pools, golf courses, tennis courts, ice-skating rinks and nightclubs—until after I was married in 1948. For our honeymoon, a week's vacation, or a weekend getaway, we'd pull out the dressy clothes that we wore at our friends' weddings and head up to a Catskill hotel. In the '50s and '60s, when our children were growing up, we introduced them to our vacation destination. Around the same time, a triple whammy—air conditioning, women going back to work, and cheap air fares—began to have an impact on the Catskills. We and many of our friends and relatives abandoned the mountains. By the time my children were teenagers, they went off to summer camp in the Berkshires and we flew off to Europe for sightseeing vacations.

Thriving villages became ghosts of their former selves, depressed and depressing. In its heydey, the area was blanketed by six hundred hotels. Today, they number fewer than twenty. By the 1990s, most had succumbed to lightning fires, bankruptcy, and the real-estate market. A few still stand as empty shells awaiting redevelopment.

More than five hundred bungalow colonies existed in the 1950s and '60s. Now about two hundred remain, some converted to co-ops. Seniors from Florida come for the summer, and some bungalows are occupied by singles seeking less expensive alternatives to the Hamptons or Fire Island. Most have been bought by Brooklyn's *haredi* (ultra-Orthodox) communities; the town of Woodbourne, my old stomping grounds, has particularly been revitalized by their presence during the summer and early autumn season. During the week, Hasidic women in long sleeves and opaque stockings can be seen strolling the hot country roads with their children. I imagine them enjoying their midweek summer break, much as my mother did, with husbands and fathers back in the city.*

* Ruth Lehrer. "Jewish Women in the Catskills" by Ruth Lehrer, Reprinted from Jewish Currents, July/August 2003.

12

Books And Reading

"Supper's ready," my mother announced. "It's on the table," she shouted a few minutes later. Finally, "It's getting cold, come in already." I could not rouse myself from my niche under the dining room table, on my belly, with a book—*The Bobbsey Twins, Nancy Drew*, or the countless others whose titles seduced me.

My parents read a Yiddish newspaper every day, but the only book we owned was my father's prayer book. From the time I learned to read in first grade, the public library became my home away from home. Without any adult guidance—family, teacher, or librarian—my book selections were a matter of chance.

A set of twins lived in my apartment building and we were good friends. When we finished playing they went off together, and I went home—alone. I was so envious of them. Imagine, having someone who looked like me, thought like me, and was always there for me to play with! The word *twins* in the title attracted me to *The Bobbsey Twins*. After I read the first one, it was like eating potato chips; I couldn't stop. I finished every volume in the series, and went on to the *Nancy Drew* mysteries, which were even more absorbing. They were my *Harry Potters*.

I didn't much care for my reading assignments in high school—*Silas Marner, The Iliad, The Odyssey, Macbeth*. At the time I thought they were boring. Besides, I was working part-time and had acquired a boyfriend. When dinner was ready, there I was, at the table, while the food was still hot. Who had time to read? A few years later, as a sophomore at City College, I found time. Sinclair Lewis, Charles Dickens, Theodore Dreiser, Henry James—mesmerizing. Poor Ma, I was hooked again.

I was back at it as a young, stay-at-home mom; lunchtime, dinnertime, bedtime—my head was in my book. Beds were left undone, clothes unwashed, meals late. In that Neverland time, I discovered Jewish writers and literature with Jewish content. Often I felt as if the authors were writing my story.

While other people were horrified at the graphic sexual content of Philip Roth's *Portnoy's Complaint*, I was fascinated with the Jewish mother-child relationship it portrayed. Roth's mother was my mother, strong willed, a "producer and promoter of guilt." I relived the Thirties' Bronx with E.L.Doctorow in *World's Fair*, as he went to P.S.70, the school in which I first began substitute teaching. Together we went to Yankee Stadium, or to his "second-floor apartment, one flight up, on West 173 Street." My own second-floor apartment, one flight up, was located near the corner of East 173 Street. In *Marjorie Morningstar*, Herman Wouk probes his nineteen-year-old heroine's psyche when she works at a resort on Schroon Lake in the Adirondacks. I was nineteen when I worked as a counselor at an adult camp on that very same lake, and I morphed into Marjorie as I read.

My sons would glance at the book in my hand as they were growing up, and tease me about it being a "Jewish" book, which it most often was. Beginning with Henry Roth in 1934, there were many emerging Jewish American authors. Roth's *Call It Sleep* is a deeply moving story of immigrant life. David, a perceptive young boy, wanders about the streets of the Lower East Side of Manhattan and sees a world filled with hate and indifference.

Our Crowd, by Stephen Birmingham, reveals a different side of Jewish society—the great Jewish banking families of New York. This insider's view of the rich and famous introduced me to German Jews like Loeb, Lehman, Straus, Lewisohn, Guggenheim, and Warburg. Now, after fifty years, I scarcely recall the details, and they've all merged into one big Jewish mogul.

When I was a youngster, Zayde, my personal storyteller, entertained me with Bible stories. My Talmud Torah teachers included them in their curriculum. As an adult I took Bible-as-literature classes in local synagogues, Elderhostel, and a retired teachers' learning center. Conversations with my brother-in-law Sam, a Jewish literature teacher, led me to view the Bible as human drama.

Reading about Eve and her predecessor, Lillith (who is not mentioned in the Bible, but in a *midrash*), generated a lengthy class discussion about their relevance to the Women's Lib movement. Reacquainting myself with Jacob, who stole his brother's birthright, allowed me to think about the Middle East conflict in a new way. From Amos to Isaiah, I heard the Prophets' cry for social justice rather than for the observance of ritual. According to George Santayana, in his *Introduction to the Ethics of Spinoza*, "The Bible is literature, not dogma."

The *Torah*, consisting of the *Five Books of Moses* plus the commentary, contains statements and principles of law and ethics, sometimes called the 613 commandments. They are in continuous dynamic change; only 271 are considered applicable today. Many different works enumerate the commandments. I read Maimonides' original list, and was bowled over by its progressive economic rules. Fair treatment of labor, sharing of the harvest with the poor, honesty in advertising, lending and borrowing, communal access to water and fishing, and ensuring accuracy of scales and weights are but a sampling.

One of my teachers (an observant Jew) introduced the class to *Who Wrote the Bible?*, by Richard E. Friedman, challenging traditional beliefs about the authorship of the world's best seller. His book exposed us to theories relating to the different segments and time periods during which those segments were written, and presented a compelling case for their human authorship. As a historical, behavioral, and literary document I consider the Bible a treasure, worthy of study.

The motivation for reading any book is greatly enhanced when I know I'll be analyzing it with other readers. In the 1980s I joined a Brandeis University National Women's Committee study group. With the assistance of book study guides prepared by Brandeis faculty, I discovered Yiddish short stories in translation, taking place in Europe prior to the Holocaust. Sholem Aleichem's Tevya story, *Hodel*, I.B. Singer's *Gimpel the Fool,* and I.L.Peretz's *Bontsha the Silent* were among the first Yiddish stories I was exposed to. Their endearing protagonists, Tevya, Gimpel, and Bontsha are all trusting souls, never protesting their lot or questioning God's ways. How can I ever forget them?

Book discussions introduce elements we may not have thought about at first glance. In *Bontsha the Silent,* for example, the study guide pointed out that we rejoice with the angels when Bontsha enters heaven and at his simple request for hot buttered rolls every morning. In discussion we came to realize that his patience and passivity represented the long-suffering masses. When looking at the story in terms of the Holocaust, we considered passivity in the face of slaughter. That's when I understood the ambiguity of the story's last line, "The prosecutor laughs aloud, a bitter laugh." I reread the story.

In Elderhostel classes I read American Jewish short stories dealing with the Jewish experience in America. In my favorite story, *The Conversion of the Jews*, by Philip Roth, I met Ozzie, a boy who always asks questions, unlike Gimpel, Tevya, and Bontsha.

"Jesus was a real person that lived like you and me," Ozzie tells his friend Itzie. "That's what (rabbi) Binder said—that he (Jesus) wasn't God, and we don't believe he is God. Jesus' mother was Mary, and his father probably was Joseph. The only way a woman could have a baby is to have intercourse with a man."

"But the *New Testament* says his real father was God," Ozzie cries to Itzie, and then repeats the question he asked the rabbi: "If God could create the heaven and earth in six days, and make all the animals and the fish and the light in six days—the light especially, why couldn't he let a woman have a baby without having intercourse?" Thus begins this humorous and powerful story. I love the short story genre, and find Jewish short stories—all peering into the Jewish soul—the most satisfying reading of all.

Once a year, Arthur and I take our turn at leading the discussion at a Friday night bi-monthly book group. The upcoming host brings in four or five books—novels or biography—and group members vote for the one they most prefer to read. One year, when it was our turn, I made a unilateral decision not to offer a choice. Instead, I distributed copies of my favorite American Jewish short stories and Yiddish stories in translation. Most people were unfamiliar with them, and very receptive. They found all of the stories intriguing, but there were too many to analyze in one evening. One story at a time would have been more productive. Members have not voted for a short story collection since, Jewish or otherwise. But it seems to me that subsequent choices have included a greater selection of books with Jewish themes.

In 1980, Aaron Lansky, a twenty-three-year-old student, set out to rescue the world's abandoned Yiddish books—and found more than a million of them! After publishing his amazing story, *Outwitting History*, in 2004, Lansky addressed a huge audience at Queens College. His book sold out by the time I got to the author's table. I intended to buy it elsewhere, but never did. So I was delighted, when four years later, *Outwitting History* was chosen by our book group. The discussion that followed considered this young man's motivation in preserving Yiddish literature. We examined our own feelings for *Yiddishkeit*, and questioned our grandchildren's commitment to its preservation. I returned my library book and finally bought a copy of my own—to share with my grandsons.

I have not read anything in Yiddish for over fifty years. Reading the *chutzpadik* adventures of this young man smitten with the language and its literature has inspired me to seek out a group that meets to read Yiddish text in its original form. It will be *my* adventure.

13

Theatre

A theatrical performance? Why not? I'm always ready to go. Procuring hugely discounted tickets from groups like ELT, TDF, HA, or Play-by-Play has empowered my habit. In 1963 I started saving the playbills. Each year I add about seventy-five new ones to my bulging files.

I was nine years old when Ma took me to my first show—in *Yiddish*. By 1885, New York had become the world capital of Yiddish theatre. In 1927, there were twenty-four Yiddish theatres across America, eleven of them in New York. It is estimated that every Yiddish-speaking adult in the city saw an average of more than three Yiddish shows a year. The plays included sentimental melodramas, quasi-historical operettas, and Judaised Shakespeare, Ibsen, or Shaw.

I can see myself looking up at the dimly lit stage in a dark cavernous theatre, enthralled by the actors who were emoting, clowning, and gesticulating. I cannot recall seeing all the great performers my mother talked about, like Aaron Lebedeff, Boris Thomashefsky, or Maurice Schwartz. I do remember seeing Molly Picon and Menashe Skulnick. I'm not sure if it's the Menashe I saw as a child, or as an adult, but the image of him starting his routine with *"Di kenst mir?"* (You know me?) is vivid, and still makes me smile.

As a young adult in the late 1940s and '50s, I lost interest in Yiddish as a language and stopped going to Yiddish theatre. By the mid '60s—when I came around to appreciating everything Yiddish—the curtain had come down on that wonderful art form. I felt like a kid with a popsicle when Joseph Papp started the *Yiddish Theater at the Public Theater* in 1989, designed to revive the disappearing genre. "It's so musical a language, perfect for the theatre," he declared. His first production, *Songs of Paradise*, produced in the tradition of a *Purimshpiel* (a satirical Purim play), was a delight. Its playbill is one of my most cherished souvenirs. "This venture is part of my commitment to quality theatre, the kind that reflects the cultural diversity of New York," Papp wrote. Alas, he died in 1991, and his venture into Yiddish theatre died with him.

In the year 2000, actress Zypora Spaisman started the *New Yiddish Public Theatre*. I had seen her perform in a Folksbiene presentation of *Green Fields* in 1974, and she chose the same play for her new company. This time she took the role of mother, not daughter. The show was charming, but I do believe that was the last venture into Yiddish Public Theatre. The *Folksbein*, at the JCC in Manhattan, is now the only major performing group still in existence.

Everything sounds funnier and more profound to me in *mameloshen*. I'm always tickled by Gilbert and Sullivan operettas, but when I witnessed a Yiddish translation of *Pirates of Penzance (Die Yam Gozlonim),* the lyrics seemed funnier than ever. I subsequently took a chance on a Town Hall presentation of *A Millionaire in Trouble*, a Yiddish Israeli comedy show starring Yakov Bodo, whom I'd never heard of. (I later learned that Bodo is one of Israel's shining lights.) I went because it was in Yiddish, and even when a Yiddish show is not great, I *kvell* at the idiomatic expressions and laugh at the stereotypical jokes.

When my sons were young we took them to two-for-one musical matinees at the Westbury Music Fair and to the monumental productions on the small stage at Equity Library Theatre. Both boys became drama counselors at summer camp. In 1970, we went to see *Story Theatre* (twice) at the Ambassador Theatre on Broadway. The creative translation of classic children's stories for a mostly adult audience was great fun, and so clever. I borrowed the idea and brought it to the fourth grade class I was teaching at the time. Instead of using prose tales, I found half a dozen long rhyming story poems and adapted them for choral speaking. *Poem Theatre*, our dramatic presentation in the auditorium at the end of the school year, was a huge success. I recall the stage, strewn with paper bags and other debris, because "Sarah Cynthia Sylvia Stout, would not take the garbage out." I continued these programs with each successive class, adding new poems along the way, until my retirement fourteen years later.

Broadway has provided me with a theatrical *Gan Eyden* (Garden of Eden) since I was a teenager. Included in their bounty was a large variety of American plays with *Jewish soul*. My most memorable dramas include: *I'm Not Rappaport, The Price, Awake and Sing, Abie's Irish Rose, The Dybbuk, The Last Night of Ballyhoo, Driving Miss Daisy, Conversations With My Father*, and *The Tenth Man*. Add to that the comedy-dramas of Neil Simon and Wendy Wasserstein. Finally, sprinkle in the few Broadway musicals that have incorporated or hinted at Jewish themes. *Fiddler on the Roof, Cabaret, Funny Girl, Chu Chem*, and *The Producers* are the ones that come to mind. I was lucky to have feasted on so many delicious offerings.

I identified with the characters, the culture, and the politics of all these plays—serious, comedic, and musical. Some featured Jewish characters, but the themes were universal. Some were poignant, some were funny. Most were provocative and insightful. Nowadays, I may come upon a review of a revival: "shallow," "dated," "a string of television sitcoms." I don't go to revivals. I want to hold on to the glowing memory of the original.

Best of all was attending the now defunct Jewish Repertoire Theatre (JRT) and the American Jewish Theatre, which dedicated themselves exclusively to the presentation of plays dealing with the Jewish American experience:

I enjoyed major new works by Howard Fast, Grace Paley, Eric Bentley, and Isaac Bashevis Singer, along with translations of some of the great Yiddish classics written by Peretz Hirshbein, Sholem Aleichem, Sholem Asch, and David Pinski, among others.

These plays often featured old-time veterans of the Yiddish stage, and included *schmaltzy* dramas and comedies like *Shlemiel The First, Success Story, Me and Molly, Crossing Delancey Street, Today I Am A Fountain Pen, Show Me Where The Good Times Are,* and *Edith Stein.*

The JRT was masterful in producing the Jewish musical. Of the many I thrilled to, those I remember best are *Pearls, The Shop on Main Street, Sophie, Kuni Leml,* and *Sheba.* The most poignant was *The Special.* It was a *mekhaye* (pleasure) to be in the audience. The demise of both production companies by the year 2000 was a major loss to New York City—and to me personally.

Years later, I spotted the petite Yiddish performer, Mina Bern, in a theatre lobby. I had seen her perform in *The Special,* and the vision of her singing *I Don't Want That You Don't Want* (referring to her grandchild's interfaith romance) flashed before me. I dashed across the crowded room. "Mina Bern?" I asked. She seemed surprised to be recognized. "I loved your performance in *The Special,*" I gushed. A huge smile lit up her face—and mine—as we conjured up those wonderful days of the Jewish Repertoire musicals, that delightful show, and that memorable song. Coupled with a bowl of barley mushroom soup and a corned beef sandwich at the Second Avenue Deli just a few blocks away, those performances were the highlight of my theatrical adventuring.

I treasure the playbills I've collected from all the "Jewish shows" I've seen, now residing in the coffers of my large antique oak filing cabinet. I refer to them more often than one would imagine. Who starred in *Me and Molly*? At what theatre did I see *Gimpel the Fool*? Was it Mina Bern or Shifra Lerer who played with Zypora Spaisman in *Green Fields*? I didn't get to see Zero Mostel as Tevya in *Fiddler on the Roof.* Who replaced him in that role? I'm adrift in a sea of nostalgia each time I research a question.

* Pirates of Penzance, *Die Yam Gozlonim*, a production of the Long Island Yiddish Gilbert and Sullivan.

14

Going To The Movies

My mother introduced me to the movies before I entered kindergarten. Admission was a dime and included free dishes on Tuesday evenings. Starting in junior high school, my friends and I spent all our Saturday afternoons in the darkened theatre, no matter what was playing. Each film— musical, comedy, or drama—was an escape from reality as I knew it. In *Love Affair*, Irene Dunne is struck down by an automobile on her way to a reunion with the man she loves, played by Charles Boyer. Oh, the agony of it, the tragedy, and the romance. The memory still tugs at my heartstrings. Except for the slapstick humor of the Three Stooges and the Ritz Brothers, I never saw a movie I didn't like.

There were no G and X ratings to guide us, and Ma didn't need to check for appropriateness. Sex on the screen was discreet, and violence almost non-existent. The physical comedy of the Three Stooges was not funny to me then, and it's not funny to me now. But today's violence is horrific—graphic, glorified, and gratuitous. I have no doubt that it is responsible for the increase of violent acts in our schools. Those films get no revenue from me.

From the beginning, Jews have been prominent in the making of movies—as writers, producers, actors, and directors—but films with Jewish content were not produced until the 1940s. While I've been much more discriminating in my movie selections as an adult, when it comes to films with Jewish themes, I feel like a kid again. I'm captivated by them all. *Gentleman's Agreement, Crossing Delancey,* and *Kadosh* stand out as my three all-time favorite Jewish movies.

The subject of anti-Semitism was very much in the forefront of my family's consciousness when I was growing up, but it was never a subject I was exposed to in the movies. *Gentleman's Agreement* (1947), the Oscar-winning adaptation of Laura Z. Hobson's novel, was the first of its kind. Gregory Peck plays a journalist who discovers rampant anti-Semitism while pretending to be Jewish. He identifies with his new persona and responds with anger, frustration, and determination to expose his findings. At the time it was a daring approach to the subject. Although the story is dated, I still find the film riveting, no matter how many times I catch a rerun on television.

How can I forget *Crossing Delancey* (1988), which I saw more than two decades ago? Amy Irving plays a sophisticated Jewish girl from Manhattan, smitten with a charming and handsome artist who has no intention of making a commitment. To the rescue comes her *bubbe* from the Lower East Side, arranging with a marriage broker to "fix her up" with a nice Jewish boy, a regular *mentsch*, the neighborhood pickle man. This heartwarming comedy contrasts our modern way of life with old-world traditions. I've played "matchmaker" many times and provided many good "dates" (even the big one leading to the altar), so I was rooting for the *bubbe*. I cry at a movie, mostly at the happy parts. The more I cry, the better the movie. I cried a lot *Crossing Delancey*.

Kadosh, an Israeli film (1999), transported me into the world of Orthodox Jews, where I became embroiled in the lives of two sisters living in an ultra-religious community in Jerusalem. Both were involved in very troubled marriages: one, cold and cruel, governed by the confines of orthodoxy; the other, genuinely loving, ripped apart by the religious injunction to be fruitful and to multiply. I was heartbroken and furious at the same time, witnessing the impact of blind faith and emotional violence portrayed in this film,

I've enjoyed so very many important movies with Jewish themes, I could not possibly comment on all of them in the format of one essay. Beginning with Marjorie Morningstar (1958), where I saw myself as Marjorie, honorable mention goes to the very best of my best, those that have been the most meaningful to me: *Exodus* (1960), *The Pawnbroker* (1964), *Bye Bye Braverman* (1968), *Goodbye, Columbus* (1969), *The Heartbreak Kid* (1972), *The Apprenticeship of Duddy Kravitz* (1974), *Hester Street* (1975), *Lies My Father Told Me* (1975), *Annie Hall* (1977), *The Chosen* (1981), *Chariots of Fire* (1981), *Shindler's List* (1993), and *A Price Above Rubies* (1998). I may not always have liked the way Jews were portrayed in these films, but the recurring themes of social currents in American Jewish society, the Holocaust, and family interaction were always honest and provocative. The violence shown in films like *Exodus* and *Shindler's List* was not presented as a virtue, but relevant to the subject.

In the year 2000, at a film retrospective in the Jewish Museum, I saw *The Goldbergs,* filmed in 1951, and later retitled—*Molly,* starring my old radio, TV, and Broadway heroine, Gertrude Berg. Berg first created *The Goldbergs,* the story of a lower-middle-class Jewish family in the Bronx, as a series of vignettes to entertain the guests at her parents' Catskill Mountain resort. In 1929, the Goldberg family made it to radio. Ma and I listened regularly from the time I was in grade school until I graduated high school in 1945.

Molly was portrayed as wise and loving, the stereotypical image of a "Jewish Mother" in that era—unlike the current *smothering* version of Jewish mothers. "Yoo-hoo, Mrs. Bloom," she sang from her kitchen window. Ma and I were besotted by her fractured English. In 1949, *The Goldbergs* moved on to television, and I fixed my eyes on Gertrude Berg for the first time. She reminded me of a big bowl of chicken soup—warm, wholesome, and full of *tom* (flavor). I hadn't known that *Molly* subsequently made it onto the big screen. There I was, half a century later, in the auditorium at the Jewish Museum, having an affectionate reunion with my old friend.

In my role as coordinator at a Jewish Studies Elderhostel program in the Catskills, I often schedule a movie after dinner, squeezing it in before the evening's nightclub entertainment. Two favorites, *Sweet Lorraine* and *Dirty Dancing*, depict life in the old Borscht Belt hotels. As an old time Catskill vacationer, the manicured grounds, hectic dining room scene, lavish food, familiar comics, hotel quandaries, and stereotypical upper-middle-class Jewish guests bring me back to another era. Talk about nostalgia.

Elderhostelers have always shared my enthusiasm for the film, *School Ties,* which I've replayed for many of the groups. David Green, a Jewish high school football star, played by Brendan Frasier, is recruited by an elite Christian prep school to boost their victories on the field. Not surprisingly, he encounters anti-Semitism and needs to make difficult ethical choices. Happily, David is not easily intimidated. Matt Damon, portraying a popular football hero expelled for cheating (after attempting to implicate David), passes him as he leaves the campus in disgrace. "I'll still get into Harvard," he says, "but you'll always be a Jew." "And you'll always be a prick," David retorts. Our audience cheers. Most of us skip the scheduled nightclub act after viewing this powerful and deeply moving motion picture. I gave a DVD of *School Ties* to my grandsons one Chanukah, and they were as captivated by it as I was.

When I see a movie with Jewish content I become totally absorbed in it, it's mine, I own it. My heart may be breaking. I may cry or get angry. But more often, there's a big smile on my face and in the core of my being.

15

Music

We had no recordings, didn't own a phonograph, television was non-existent. The voices of "Yussele" or "Leibele" or "Moishe,"* my father's cantorial superheroes, emanated from WEVD on our kitchen radio. These three famous cantors (and nameless others) provided the music I grew up with. I never became an aficionado, but by constant exposure I grew to appreciate what I called "my father's music."

I was twelve years old when Uncle Benny revealed that his neighbor was disposing of an old mahogany upright. I yearned to play the piano, to make beautiful music, and for a moment I dared to hope. Some of my friends had been taking lessons, and I loved the pieces I heard them practicing—*La Donna e mobile, Blue Danube, Humoresque, Tit Willow*—melodies I'd never heard before. But Ma was adamant—our apartment was already overcrowded, and paying for lessons was out of the question. A piano was not to be.

As a teenager I found solace and great joy in the Big Band strains of Artie Shaw, Benny Goodman, Tommy Dorsey, Harry James, and Glenn Miller—tuning in to WNEW's *Hit Parade* on Saturday nights. I danced the Lindy-Hop to *Chatanooga Choo Choo* and stood on line at the Paramount to hear Frank Sinatra. Not until my junior year at City College did I get to hear my first classical concert—under the stars in the now legendary Lewisohn Stadium.

When I was a senior, and student teaching in a Bronx elementary school, I chose to prepare a music lesson for my last scheduled observation, my grand finale. I wasn't overly confident, didn't play an instrument, never took a professional music lesson. With my supervisor sitting in the rear of the classroom, my fourth graders and I improvised a musical scale using eight drinking glasses filled with various amounts of water. I held my breath when they took turns using this "instrument" to play simple tunes—*Three Blind Mice* or *Twinkle Twinkle Little Star.* My learned professor rose to his feet and applauded.

I graduated, started teaching, married Arthur, helped him assemble an audio disc recorder/turntable, bought my first record—gave birth to a white-haired baby boy. Every evening, after his bottle, our newborn had us wringing our hands over his prolonged crying spells. What to do? Burping him was not the solution, and it was almost a month before we noticed that whenever we played a record he'd stop crying. Not just any record—Beethoven. Not just

Beethoven, but his *Fifth Symphony*. After a while, we were convinced that our infant was actually chanting the notes, "da, da, da, daaa," signaling us to play it for him!

My longing to play the piano never diminished. One week after my second son was born I bought myself a new blonde oak console piano, hired the best teacher I could find, and set out to learn *Brahms' Lullaby*. I practiced two hours a day, sometimes three, but too soon I learned that practicing did not make perfect. I had no talent. The music I created never stopped a baby from crying. But that piano became the foundation for my children's excursion into music, and the hub around which we gathered when Arthur's more talented relatives sat down to play.

Our new baby was not yet talking when I rescued a collection of old classical 78 RPMs from our neighbor's trash. Arthur resuscitated a discarded phonograph, and we bequeathed the records to our toddler. For many hours every day, along with an uncooked stick of spaghetti that he used as a baton, we'd see him plop the needle onto a shiny black disc, and rhythmically wave his arms to the music. He'd never seen an orchestra perform, but he sure looked like Toscanini.

With two such musical geniuses in our midst, we flooded our home with music. Our children's toy chests were filled with maracas, tom-toms, tambourines, castanets, a variety of recorders, and a ukulele. The boys took lessons—piano, flute, guitar. As teenagers, the records they bought were mostly rock, then jazz, followed by the minimalist music of Steve Reich and Philip Glass. We introduced them to musical theatre, and they'd listen to show tunes as well. Both sons became disc jockeys on their college radio stations. To this day music permeates their lives. Recently, they attended the American Composers Orchestra at Carnegie Hall, a Paul Simon concert at BAM, and a Philip Glass opera at the Met—all in one week. Plant some seeds and they will blossom.

When Arthur and I were a young couple looking to join a synagogue, we "auditioned" the cantors, then chose the temple with the very best. It was a no-contest competition. Cantor Bob Abelson had performed with the New York City Opera and went on to sing in Jewish musical theatre. Some members of the congregation wanted a full-time cantor. Others like me, reveling in his magnificent baritone voice, were content with his limited presence. Each son's Bar Mitzvah service, shortly before Cantor Abelson decided to leave the temple, was an operatic delight. Their grandfather was in cantorial heaven. "As good as Yussele or Lebele or Moishe," he declared.

I've attended "Three-Cantor" concerts (modeled on those by the "Three Tenors") and purchased a few cantorial recordings. My most recent acquisition is a tape of Cantor Dudu Fisher, who also played Jean Val Jean in *Les Miserables* on Broadway. Sometimes he infuses the melodic strains of *Les Ms.* into his cantorial renditions. I don't imagine a *maven* (authority) like my father would have approved, but it tickles me.

I heard my mother chanting old Yiddish tunes when she was well into her nineties, yet I cannot conjure up a vision of her singing to me as a child. But she must have, because Yiddish folk songs have been *ungebaken in hartz* (baked into my heart) for as long as I can remember. Wading through my recordings I find *Great Yiddish Melodies* (Sol Zim), *Mamaloshen* (Mandy Patimkin), *World of Jewish Folk Music* (Laura Wetzler), *Zei Gezunt* (Mickey Cohen), and *Sha Shtil* (Mark Levy)—music for the soul. An inventory of my CD collection reveals my love affair with hand clapping, foot stomping *Klezmer*. Clarinetist Giora Feidman, performing a wedding dance or a Chassidic tune makes my heart beat a little faster. Yitzhak Perlman's *Theme from Schindler's List* and Sophie Tucker's rendition of *My Yiddishe Mama* turn me into a rag doll. They all qualify for Divine Moment awards in my life.

How about Bruce Adler,** Mike Burstyn, and Avi Hoffman, the three Jewish cabaret *tummlers?* I love those song-and-dance men. Look for me in the audience when any one of them is performing in the New York area. Their Yiddish songs and adaptations—*Ich Bin A Boarder Bay Mayn Vayb, Hu-Tsa-Tsa, Rumania Rumania, Mein Shtetele Belz, Borscht Riders in the Sky,* and *Rozhinkes Mit Mandlen*—keep me on a high for days.

When my grandson, Shaineh Punim, was six years old, he became addicted to the Passover melody *Dayenu*. I'd play it for him over and over again, each time needing to find its exact place on the tape—an exercise in masochism. What won't a grandma do for her grandchild? Devising a way to keep him happy, and exposing him to my favorite folk songs at the same time, I got Grandpa into the act.

He recorded six copies of *Dayenu* onto a tape, interspersing each of them with one of my most lively, tuneful classic Yiddish or Hebrew melodies—*Az De Rebbe Geyt, Tsena-Tsena, Haleluya, Tumbelalaika,* and *Hava Nagila.* Whenever my grandson came to visit that year he'd ask for the *Dayenu* tape, and together we'd listen—clapping and swaying. I patted myself on the back when I saw his beaming face.

By the following Passover, however, he had lost interest. Rock groups like Deep Purple, and Queen, singing songs like *Smoke on the Water* and *We Will Rock You,* were now more appealing to him. He was bored with his *Dayenu,* and not at all inspired by my Yiddish favorites. So now Shaineh Punim's recording is mine alone, and I clap and I sway—on my own.

* Yussele Rosenblatt, Lebele Waldman, Moishe Oysher.
** Bruce Adler died on July 28, 2008, three months after I saw him perform at the Queens Theatre in the Park. He was 63 years old.

16

The Cruise

It was a hot July day in 1969 when we embarked on a two-week cruise to the even hotter Caribbean, our first trip outside the continental USA. Eddie, the dock supervisor, a friend of a friend, met us at our Greek-line ship and told us he had spoken with the bursar and the ship's captain. "You'll be well taken care of," he promised. I wasn't quite sure what he meant.

On deck, as the ship pulled away from shore, a tall, nattily dressed, distinguished-looking man, probably in his late fifties, caught my attention. He was a commanding figure, and I wondered who he could be—star of a TV soap, perhaps? He disappeared into the crowd, and I started a conversation with a cheerful couple from the Bronx, Estelle and Albie, who invited us to share their table in the dining room. It turned out to be a good move for all of us.

During dinner that first night, the maitre d' introduced himself and informed us that he'd be taking our special dinner requests each day. The menu listed dozens of entrée choices, many of them enticing Greek specialties— moussaka, kalamarakia, oktapodaki; the variety was dazzling. We thanked him, but declined his offer. He insisted. *Hmm, so that's what Eddie meant!* Estelle and Albie suggested beef Wellington. Arthur conjured up my mother's *kasha varnishkes* and her *vrenikes*, stuffed with garlicky potatoes, but didn't have the *chutzpah* to ask for it. The only gourmet off-menu items I could think of were baby lamb chops and lobster tails. Can you imagine getting tired of lobster? We did.

Telling humorous stories became a routine accompaniment to our elegant dining. Estelle and I, both schoolteachers, exchanged old teacher jokes. I recalled hearing about a substitute teacher who circulated an attendance sheet for her students to sign, then discovered there was one name too many on the list. Substitutes were known targets, so she deduced that someone had signed in for a buddy who was cutting class. She called off the names, one by one, arriving at Dick Hertz, a name to which no one responded. The class began to snicker. "Who's Dick Hertz?" she asked again, raising her voice. Snickering turned into loud guffawing. "Aha! I've got the culprit now," she thought, repeating her question, until she finally realized the nature of the hoax. Laughter and lobster—the four of us felt lucky to have found each other.

People thought we were old friends. On days in port we went sight-seeing together—hiring a guide and sharing a cab. Estelle suggested entering the ship's costume contest as characters from the *Wizard of Oz*. When we weren't touring, you could find us in the sewing room, turning scraps of fabric and crepe paper into masterly garments for a lion, a scarecrow, and a young girl from Kansas. The kitchen provided Estelle with large juice cans, and they became the arms and legs for her tin-man costume. I suggested singing *We're off to See the Wizard* and dancing the Jesse Polka as we entered the ballroom on the night of the contest. Estelle's tin arms and legs rattled as we practiced the dance.

From time to time I noticed my distinguished-looking mystery man weaving in and out of the crowd. Could he be an FBI agent?

A large and noisy bunch of passengers gathered on the top deck one morning to participate in an emergency ship evacuation drill. No one seemed to be in charge. People refused to get into the lifeboats. Confusion reigned. That's when I spotted my soap star/ FBI agent once again. He picked up a phone, asked for the ship's captain, told him there was an emergency, and requested him to appear on deck immediately. My hero. This was certainly a take-charge person, a corporate CEO for sure.

Formal, engraved invitations to dine with the captain were slipped under our cabin doors one day. Estelle thought it was charm and good humor that earned us that honor. I believed Eddie was at the bottom of it. No matter, we loved the attention. There were eight diners at our large round table: the captain and his wife, the four of us, and you guessed it—my mystery man and his wife. The place card next to mine revealed his identity—Rabbi Richard Hertz! I couldn't believe that Dick Hertz was my dinner-dance partner for the evening. I refrained from laughing out loud.

The rabbi may have been a take-charge person, but he was an uninspired dancer. The *rebbetzin* had a better deal, with my husband as her partner. As the two of us stumbled around the dance floor, I learned that my partner led a large congregation in Detroit and had been in the same graduating class as my rabbi in Flushing. Had I attended *Shabbes* services on board, the mystery I conjured up would have been solved so much sooner.

The next day Richard Hertz had a gleeful "reunion" with his old classmate when I showed him a photo of my rabbi, taken with my younger son at his recent Bar Mitzvah. "My friend has gained a little weight," he chuckled. I wondered if he had heard the Dick Hertz story, but decided that yes, of course he had; he must have taken lots of ribbing throughout the years.

The big night arrived. Contestants gathered outside the large ballroom, funky and colorful in their creative ship-made attire, waiting to be called. When it was our turn, we entered with a flourish, arms linked, tin cans clanking, dancing the *Jesse Polka* and singing the *Wizard* song. There was a huge uproar from the audience when we concluded our performance. Behind a bare rectangular table sat the judges—the ship's captain and the rabbi—deliberating. Third Prize, Second Prize, First Prize, the loud speaker blared.

Where were we? Estelle, Albie, and Arthur looked at each other in disappointment, their mouths open. I grinned, confidently. Another huge uproar flooded the room—the sound of protest—seconds before the final announcement. The totally impartial judges stood up and awarded us a hastily improvised Grand Prize: a *tchochke* lover's delight— a potpourri of Greek souvenirs from the gift shop!

I smile whenever I think of that Caribbean cruise, the puzzle pieces locking neatly into place. Looking back on the Captain's dinner, I no longer believe it was Eddie's influence that prompted the invitation. I know I was chosen because I was a *Yiddishe Maidel,* a Jewish dinner-dance partner for the soap star, FBI agent, CEO—turned rabbi.

RELIGION AND RITUAL

17

God

I awoke early one morning when I was five, began cutting out dolls and snowflakes from scraps of paper, then remembering it was *Shabbes*, suddenly started to cry *M'tor Nit* (thou shalt not) *use scissors on Shabbes*. There were lots of *M'tor Nits* on *Shabbes*, all mandated by God. Who was God? What was God? Why could I cut my paper dolls all week, but not on *Shabbes*? No one ever explained it to me, and now, seventy five years later, I'm still searching for answers.

My brother went to *shul* with my father. As a girl, I was not expected to go, except for *Simchas Torah* and a few family Bar Mitzvahs—all chanted in Hebrew. I was able to read the Hebrew prayers, but didn't understand what I was reading. When I began attending temple as an adult, I was confronted with the practice of responsive reading by the congregants—in English. I felt like an outsider, encountering a new religion.

God our Father, God our strength, God our King.
God our Lord, how excellent is Thy name in all the earth.
Thou shalt love the Lord, thy God, with all thy heart, with
*   all thy soul, and with all thy might.*
Who is like unto Thee, O Lord, among the mighty?

Were these the words my father and brother had been chanting all these years? And was this the same God I never was taught to love, but whom I feared on *Shabbes* when I could not cut paper into dolls?

Who is like unto Thee, glorious in holiness, awe-inspiring,
*   working wonders?*

"Awe-inspiring? Working wonders?" That's not the God I'd ever heard about. I recalled the holiday stories I learned in Talmud Torah, about Jews who were persecuted and killed. Except for a few *bubbe-meisehs*—unbelievable fairy tales like the parting of the seas—was it not individuals, people like Mordecai or Judith, who used their wiles to save the Jews, or the might of the Maccabees, who saved the temple from destruction?

I hadn't given much thought to God since dealing with the *M'tor Nits* of my childhood, and I could not actively participate in a temple service, could not utter the alien words I did not feel. Instead, I used the time searching for nuggets of truth and wisdom in the Reform prayer book. On Yom Kippur I read:

We sin when we are indifferent to the plight of our neighbors,
and seek only our own welfare; when we permit ourselves to
be ignorant; when we cast into the waste-heap the precious
heritage of our people.

We ask forgiveness for turning our intelligence into an instru-
ment of death to others and to ourselves; for our tragic belief
that power makes for happiness; for robbing and plundering
the earth; for our unhappy world to which each of us has
imparted his own measure of folly and sin.

These are the lines that resonated with me—*we people*, taking responsibility for our own actions. There are many such nuggets, so fresh and so relevant, that each time I read them I feel like I'm seeing them for the first time. I enjoy being in a Jewish edifice, surrounded by Jewish people, partaking in a Jewish event, embracing Jewish values. It doesn't have much to do with worshipping God.

The Ten Commandments tell me that God determines what happens on earth and that the good will be rewarded. My brother was thirty-nine when he took ill and died. His youngest child was six, his oldest thirteen. He was the wisest, handsomest, best person I knew—and a committed synagogue member. "It's God's Will," a friend whispered, in an effort to comfort me. I felt like I'd been stabbed. Why would God will such a thing?

God's Will—after the Holocaust many people could no longer tolerate that concept. How could God have allowed such a thing to happen? They needed a different interpretation of how God works. One rationale is that God suffers along with the victims; "free-will" is another. Most recently I heard a third: The Holocaust had to happen in order for the state of Israel to be born. This last one serves to keep intact the traditional view of an all-powerful deity. None of the rationales work for me.

Scientists, philosophers, and ordinary people like me have been contemplating the nature of God throughout the centuries. My book group voted to read *Betraying Spinoza*, by philosopher Rebecca Goldstein,* a departure from our usual fiction or biographical choices. I knew that Spinoza, a seventeenth-century Dutch Jew, had been excommunicated for his ungodly beliefs—but that was all I knew. Delving into the book I was surprised to learn how great a part God did play in his life. (Some people have even called him *God-intoxicated*.) I found his philosophy to be more intriguing than I expected, and more complex.

The way I understand it, Spinoza believed that "rigorous reason" was essential before coming to any conclusions; that God and *nature* were one and the same; that religious dogma was an impediment to the understanding of nature. I'd like to be a student in Goldstein's course on this iconic figure.

Because of his "evil opinions and monstrous deeds," the Portuguese Jewish community of *Marranos* in Amsterdam officially excommunicated, expelled, cursed, and damned Baruch de Espinoza—"with the consent of God." He was twenty-three years old and had not yet written a word. Christian Europe agreed with the Jews that Spinoza was a heretic and an atheist.

Does searching for the meaning of God make one a heretic or an atheist? Life is a quest. My-Son-the-Artist recognizes "the beauty, design, and paradox of the universe," and sees "God in everyone and everything." His is a spiritual vision, not a religious one. My-Son-the-Journalist thinks "religious experiences and opinions about God probably come from the cultural, psychological, and biochemical, not the supernatural," but he doesn't know for sure. How is it possible for anyone to know for sure?

The renowned Orthodox scholar and social critic, Rabbi Adin Steinsalz, writes:

> "Whatever we do, we will never be able to comprehend God. . . . the Almighty Himself is far beyond anything that even the most sublime human mind can comprehend." He goes on to say that the Torah and its commandments, the divine Revelation on Mount Sinai, ". . . reveals to us the way to actually unite with God, namely, by fulfilling his commandments."**

I heartily endorse the Torah's message of communal responsibility, but I do not accept its divine origin. Therefore, I agree with Steinsalz: whatever I do, I will never be able to comprehend God—the way he does.

My thinking is that we mortals created God—all-good and all-powerful—for our own comfort. God is a concept, conceived to explain the inexplicable. I cannot fathom why my view of God would matter to anyone else. But it has mattered—throughout history. In the name of God, religious extremists have expelled, persecuted, and killed those whose concept of God differs from their own. Incomprehensible!

On the other hand, current anti-God authors warn us of "The God Delusion," or to "Beware of God," and that "Religion Poisons Everything." It seems to me that railing against God is almost as bad as declaring death to the infidel. If God provides solace and satisfies needs, it's okay with me. Part of me is envious of the faith people have. Studies have shown that there is a correlation between centenarians and belief in God. It would make life so much easier, and maybe even healthier, if I could just go along with it.

I may not believe in Steinsalz' Almighty, all-powerful, all-knowing supernatural God, but God and I do have a relationship. "*Oh my God,*" I think, when I've been mulling over a question and serendipitously find the answer in a random page of a random magazine I've picked up in a physician's office. *Oh-my-God*-moments arise when I hear bad news, great news, or witness a breathtakingly majestic scene at the beach.

When someone sneezes I instinctively shout, "*Gezuntheit,*" not, "*God bless you.*" But without thinking, I may say, "*God forbid,*" contemplating a possible disaster, and "*For God's sake,*" when I'm annoyed. "*Thank God,*" I declare, upon hearing of a missing child who has been found and is back home with her parents. When something or someone comes along that is healing or liberating I call it a "*Godsend.*" Sometimes I add "*God willing*" when making an appointment.

God knows these are all meaningful expressions. In them God represents the unknowable, the miraculous, the awesome. Spinoza called it *nature*. Whatever I call it, or don't call it, I know I remain grateful and respectful of the opportunity to ponder It, Him, Her. . . .

---

* Rebecca Goldstein. Betraying Spinoza, Random House, 2006.
** Rabbi Adin Steinsaltz. "The Torah As God's Gift," The Jewish Week, May 18, 2007. Rabbi Adin Steinsaltz is an author, scholar, and social critic best known for his monumental translation of and commentary on the Talmud.

18

Religion-Heavy; Religion-Lite

Eyebrows have been raised. A secular Jew like me lighting *Shabbes* candles, keeping kosher, and attending High Holiday services? Some people have called it hypocritical. I call it *religion-lite*.

Throughout history people have been predisposed to religious adherence. Yet the most vitriolic words have been spoken and the world's worst atrocities committed, all in the name of religion. *Religion-lite* may be hypocritical, but what we need to be worried about is *religion-heavy*.

In Europe, Pope Urban II personally promoted the first Holy Crusade in 1096, "led by God himself," to reclaim the Holy Land from the infidel Turks. The **Christian Crusades** lasted 250 years and slaughtered whole communities of Jews in Worms, Mainz, and across Europe. **The Inquisition,** started by Pope Innocente III to expose Christian heretics in the last years of the twelfth century, lasted 350 years.

It was extended to include *conversos* (Jews who converted to Christianity) and eventually to all Jews in Spain and Portugal. Rebecca Goldstein, historian and philosopher, author of *Betraying Spinoza*, reveals long nights of violence against Jews, bogus trials, forced conversions, exile, torture, group massacres, and mass burnings at the stake. Some Jews were sold as slaves to the Moslems. *Now that's what I call religion-heavy.*

Increasingly, *religion-heavy* in the United States has escalated to the point of concern. When I take a look at the media I see that the Christian Right has bought up all available radio and television stations in this country. Their agenda: radical conservative politics. The Yurica Report writes that it is the largest communications network in the world.* Speaking to a convention of religious broadcasters, conservative activist Phyllis Schlafly stated, "Give your listeners the daily news through the eyes of those who believe in God."

In the year 2000, the Christian Right (considered the base of the Republican Party) elected George W. Bush to the presidency. In 2003, when journalist Bob Woodward asked the president if he had consulted his father before invading Iraq, President Bush replied, "He is the wrong father to appeal to in terms of strength. There is a higher father that I appeal to." In 2005, the BBC reported that President Bush, speaking to Palestinian ministers, declared that God advised him to invade Iraq.

Televangelist Pat Robertson branded 9/11 "God's punishment for America's sins." On his TV show, the "700

Club," he and Reverend Jerry Falwell placed the blame for the attack on pagans, abortionists, feminists, gays, and lesbians. Christian schools like Regent University were founded to provide "Christian leadership to change the world." Many of their graduates were given jobs in the Bush administration.

New York Times columnist Paul Krugman writes, "The infiltration of the federal government by large numbers of people seeking to impose a religious agenda—which is very different from simply being people of faith –is one of the most important stories of the last six years."** It is not only an important story, it is a scary story. Their agenda and ascent to power in this country is unprecedented.

Yet the Christian Right is outspoken in their support of the state of Israel and the settlements. The Ontario Consultants on Religious Tolerance report that ever since Christ's death, most Fundamentalists and other conservative Christians have been expecting the second coming [in Palestine]. Called the *Rapture*, it "will occur when Christ first returns towards earth. Most believe that Christ will not actually land or stay on earth at this time; the 'real' second coming will occur later, when he returns on a horse leading an army on horseback who will exterminate one third of the earth's population in a massive genocide."*** How's that for *religion-heavy?* I don't think that Jesus, the Jew, could ever have imagined such a scenario, all conceived in his name.

In spite of the Fundamentalist agenda, many observant Jews welcome their support. Some Jews believe the second coming is a precursor to the arrival of the Messiah. The way I figure it, most of them don't believe in the *Rapture*, don't believe it will ever happen, so what the heck? In an increasingly hostile world, they'll take all the support they can get. Strange bedfellows, I'd say.

Several recently published books suggest that the world would be a better place if organized religion would miraculously disappear. I may not find my Jewish identity in religious belief or religious practice, but I find a balance in *religion-lite*—partaking in selective ceremonies and rituals that affirm my identity and give me a sense of belonging. Ritual could be seen as a way to define oneself as a committed Jew and to achieve the highest level of one's being. I don't believe that my observances make me a better person or define me as a better Jew. They connect me to my Jewishness and make me feel good.

This essay was conceived as a response to secular friends and relatives who have questioned my *religion-lite* practices—carrying on the traditions of my childhood. Secular Christians still set up a Christmas tree each year. Descendants of *conversos*, Jews converted to Christianity during the Spanish Inquisition more than five hundred years ago, are often Catholics, who light candles on Friday nights, keep meat and dairy separate, and don't work on Saturdays—just like me. The long arm of heritage and habit triumphs.

Irving Howe, author of *World of Our Fathers*, compared "*religion-lite*" to "weak tea." Personally, I like my tea weak. It's comforting and doesn't irritate my system. Secular

Jews who eschew *religion-lite* partake in their family *seders* or *Chanukah* parties. If they were to examine their activities closely, they too would probably discover remnants of a ritual or a Jewish rite of passage they hang on to—circumcision, bar mitzvah, sitting *shivah*, fasting on *Yom Kippur*, affixing a *mezuzah* to the doorpost, or buying wholesale. I'll order up my religion on rye, with mustard, a sour pickle, and a Dr. Brown's Cel-Ray soda.

* Katherine Yurica. www.yuricareport.com.
** Paul Krugman. "For God's Sake," New York Times, April 13, 2007.
*** "What is the Rapture?" Ontario Consultants on Religious Tolerance. RelgiousTolerance.org.

19

Shabbes

"I'm a Sabbath observer," I told a friend. Her eyebrows lifted in disbelief. Hadn't we driven to a library musical the previous Saturday? Observers do not drive on the Sabbath. Traditionally, it is a day of rest and prayer. But it is also a day of joy and pleasure, a day apart. Since childhood, *Shabbes* has been different from all other days.

On Friday nights I usher in the Sabbath when I recite the prayer over the candles, the lovely ceremony I watched as a child and observed with my mother during the last fifteen years of her life. Ma lived in a senior residence four blocks from my home. Most Friday nights I'd be there promptly at sundown, for that's when she'd drape a lace shawl over her white hair and wave her hands over the three candles in her silver candelabra, and together we'd chant,

Baruch Atah Adonai Elohanu Melech Ha'alom Asher Kidshanu Barmitzvotov Vitzivonu L'hadlik Ner Shel-Shabbat.

So now, on those Friday nights when I'm home, I do the same—and Ma is with me. Then I go off to play bridge or to a book discussion—a restful, joyous, and pleasurable beginning to the best twenty-four hours of my week.

In my parents' home, the difference between *Shabbes* and all other days was in some ways sharply delineated, in others, ambiguous. I was expected to conform to a list of Shabbes *M'tor Nits* (Thou Shalt Nots):

M'tor Nit: ride the elevator, listen to the radio, phone a friend, or turn on the lights.

M'tor Nit: cut or sew doll clothing, throw a ball, or shoot immies.

M'tor Nit: handle money, not even to buy a cherry-filled chocolate, my daily treat. I followed a list of meaningless rules; the silliest was not to tear toilet tissue. God was watching.

I knew what I was not supposed to do. But what was I allowed to do? From Monday to Friday I went to school, played with my friends, did homework, and listened to the radio. Sunday was family day—aunts, uncles, cousins; apple strudel, *ruggelach*, cheese blintzes. But on Saturday, nothing was defined. My father went to *shul*. My mother dressed up in her *Shabbes* finery and read the *Forward*. What did the mandate for a day of rest mean for me?

It was evident, since no one stopped me, that reading was acceptable. So, in my best dress and new shoes, I spent the day finishing my latest Nancy Drew mystery or Bobbsey

Twin adventure. Alone, or with a friend, I explored the other Bronx—Crotona Park and Bronx Park—the one without pavement, with grass and trees, flowers and birds. Maybe God's residence was not my home after all, hovering over a roll of toilet tissue.

When I was sixteen, *Shabbes* took on a new element of wonder. After all, at that age a girl was ready for courtship and marriage, and Ma, progressively distancing herself from orthodoxy, began taking me shopping to the budget department stores, S.Klein's and Ohrbachs, on Union Square. She wouldn't shop for the household, but she violated quite a few *M'tor Nits*, riding the subway, pursuing fashion bargains, and paying for lunch at the Horn and Hardart Automat. In doing so, she released me from the bondage of Thou Shalt Nots and allowed me to make my own choices for observing the day.

I maintain a pattern of frenetic activity and obligatory tasks all week, while *Shabbes* remains a day apart, a day for relaxation. It's the day I find time to spend a few hours answering my e-mails and editing my latest essay. What is more spiritual than the joy of creation? Like a slow Tango, the day unfolds, as I shed my everyday skin, sleeping late perhaps, styling my hair, doing Yoga stretches. It's the day for reading—wading through a sea of accumulated magazines or finishing up last week's *Jewish Week*. Arthur and I go for a walk at Little Bay Park or on the boardwalk at Jones Beach. We go into Manhattan for a Broadway matinee or to a museum exhibit. The Jewish Museum, traditionally closed on Saturdays, has opened its doors to the public—for *Shabbes* observers like me. Best of all are the days I spend visiting my children and grandchildren, on those off-season Saturdays when Little League is in recess.

Listening to Jonathon Schwartz play Frank Sinatra on WNYC and phoning a friend who has moved to Florida do not represent blasphemy. Chores do. Drudgery does. I do not go marketing. I do not sort bills or write checks. I do not cook or clean house. And I try not to dwell on what is happening in the Middle East. It is forbidden to disturb the joy of this day with dark and baleful thoughts. I have imposed upon myself a list of *Shabbes M'tor Nits*.

While in attendance at a recent *Shabbes* meeting of the Queens Community for Cultural Judaism, I heard a new prayer recited over the lighting of the Sabbath candles:

We rejoice in our heritage which gives us the tradition of lighting the Sabbath candles.

Short. Sweet. Good. I identified with it immediately. It was more meaningful to me than the Hebrew prayer I say each week.

But the Hebrew prayer over the lighting of the candles is my *mantra*. I have never given thought to the literal meaning of its words. The syllables trip easily and liltingly as I chant them from memory, ingrained since childhood. Such is the nature of ritual, which is not rational, or rooted in belief, but continues to play a part in the *Yiddishkeit* I feel. I will probably go on chanting the traditional Hebrew blessing forever.

20

Food

Mother's milk was not the food that gave me sustenance. Ma was committed to healthy eating, but much to her dismay, the best she could do was to fill my baby bottle with Sheffield's Grade A, or freshly squeezed orange juice flavored with nutrient-laden cod liver oil. Committed also to home cooking, she rejected Mrs. Gerber's revolutionary new baby food and prepared her own pureed fruits and vegetables. When I was old enough, she sliced tiny slivers of first-cut baby lamb chops, and mashed de-boned white fish into creamed carrots. Unintentionally, she was setting me up to becoming the picky eater I am today.

Money was always tight, and Ma looked for bargains in everything she bought—except for food. *"When you shop for food you get what you pay for."* Buying *kosher* was to buy the best, the highest quality. *Keeping kosher* by separating *flaishik* (meat) and *milchik* (dairy), and salting meat to preserve it meant she was providing the healthiest meals she could.

From the time I was a bride, I honored my mother's traditions by buying kosher food products. I kept *four* sets of dishes: two sets *flaishik* and two sets *milchik*—utilitarian crockery for everyday use, delicate china for guests. I also included four sets of cutlery. When my children were teenagers, I injured my ankle, and Ma came to help out, bringing along her own food supply. She did not trust my home to be kosher enough! When she left, I bought a package of bacon and cooked it up in a large frying pan. Never again would I keep a kosher household. After all, wasn't I keeping kosher for her? It was not long before I came to realize that I was also doing it for myself, that it had become an integral part of me. I threw away the pan and returned my kitchen to its former "kosher" status.

Outside my home, I did not concern myself with eating kosher, but I maintained my mother's injunction not to mix meat with dairy, and not to eat pork or ham, because they came from a pig, "a dirty animal." Yet, as a teenager, my friends ordered bacon and tomato sandwiches—and so did I. I was truly unaware that bacon came from that "dirty animal." As couples on dates, we ate knishes and pastrami in a kosher delicatessen, and spare ribs in a Chinese restaurant. My mother served *rib* steak all the time, so it didn't occur to me that spare ribs came from a pig! To this day I continue to avoid ham or anything labeled pork, like pork chops or roast pork, and to avoid mixing meat with dairy. Ice cream for dessert when I eat spare ribs? Ugh!

By the time my sons graduated from college, red meat and poultry had been eliminated from the family diet. Although we ate fish, we called ourselves vegetarians. No longer did I need separate sets of dishes or silverware. To this day I consider my home to be kosher. Out come the paper goods when I serve take-out barbecued chicken to invited guests. People have called my kosher/ non-kosher habits "irrational." They are. Aren't most religious practices? I call it *religion-lite*.

Starting around the same time, I became a *healthnik*, known also as a Health Nut. As Danny Kaye once said, "What should I be, a Sick Nut?" I was juggling a variety of physical symptoms, scheduling appointments with a variety of doctors, who prescribed a variety of medications, which caused a variety of new symptoms. There had to be another way. By listening to "alternative" medical people on radio and reading a wide range of health newsletters and magazines my focus became "natural healing," with an emphasis on diet and nutritional supplements. My experiment with a macrobiotic diet (grains, beans, fruits and vegetables) didn't last too long. I missed my protein fix of eggs, fish, and cheese.

Not until I was sixty-five did I learn that the digestive symptoms I'd experienced since I was a teenager were due to celiac disease—an intolerance to gluten—misdiagnosed for half a century! I was relieved to learn that the only prescribed treatment was eliminating all gluten-containing food (wheat, rye, and barley). A natural healing cure? Bring it on! I heard Gary Null, my radio health guru, declare that gluten stuffs your belly and clouds your brain. I was already on a low-fat, low-sugar, and low-salt diet. Cutting out gluten didn't seem like such a big deal.

How wrong I was. At my cousin's Bar Mitzvah, trays of tempting franks-in-a-blanket, assorted *knishes,* and mini *potato latkes* passed me by—all forbidden. Was there anything I could eat? Most specialty foods at traditional Jewish celebrations are made with gluten-containing ingredients. How does a Jewish girl survive without *kasha varnishkes, blintzes,* or *lukshen kugel,* the soul food she was raised on?

My cousin invited me for Rosh Hashanah dinner, to be brought in from her neighborhood kosher caterer. Eating at home is easy. Eating out, aye, that's the problem. Celiacs need to ask questions, and this was no exception. "What do you know about the chopped liver?" I began, a lawyer, prodding a reluctant witness. Did it contain bread crumb fillers? What about the brisket? Contents of gravy unknown, thickened with flour, no doubt. Clearly, the chicken had been dusted with something—glutenous, of course. Matzah balls? Forget about it. *Yiddishe maidel,* no more *knaidel*!

My cousin was not too happy when I retrieved her "home-made" chicken soup can from the garbage pail. The label verified my suspicions. Luckily, I had contributed some gluten-free gefilte fish loaves, sliced carrots, and a couple of apples, to be dipped into honey. When the *challah* was cut, I pulled out my trusty rice cakes. Nowadays, I donate a platter of roasted vegetables when I'm invited to dinner. I don't go home hungry, but I won't say that I never feel deprived.

These health conscious days, Arthur and I don't eat out much. We work as a team; I do the slicing, he does the dicing. We put together simple, yet delicious gluten-free, low-everything, fish and vegetable meals. Ma taught me well—no heartburn from her Jewish cooking. I follow her recipes for split pea soup, kasha, and salmon loaf. Favorite-Son-in-Law sautés Swiss chard or kale with garlic and olive oil, and serves it with kidney beans and Basmati rice. Most days I feast on a bowl of blueberries, just like I did when I was a kid during summer vacations.

I remember those mornings in the Catskills. Ma and I, carrying a couple of beach buckets, would wander into the woods bordering our bungalow colony and pluck the largest *huckleberries* we could find, racing to see who would pick the most before succumbing to the noonday heat. I usually won. I don't think Ma would be surprised to learn that along with Omega-3 cod liver oil, her berries have made it to the very top of the health food gurus' hit parade.

Although the use of synthetic pesticides in the United States began in the 1930s, I know those many gallons of berries we picked were wild and pure. Today, I use very little processed food and buy *organic** fruits and vegetables whenever possible. Conventionally grown produce is less expensive, but there's no doubt in my mind what Ma would choose. *"When you shop for food you get what you pay for."*

* Organic food must meet specified production standards.

21

Christmas

December 1930s. Santa Claus appeared around town and in the toy section of department stores. Trees twinkled in store fronts and behind curtained windows. *Deck the Halls* permeated the atmosphere. Christmas was coming, the birthday of Jesus Christ, and I wasn't invited to his party. Just thinking of him terrified me.

My parents grew up in Eastern European ghettoes. The Christian community blamed the Jews for Jesus' death, and he was at the core of the horror stories my mother told—discrimination, persecution, and pogroms directed at Jews. And so Christmas, the glitzy celebration of Jesus' birthday, became a scary forbidden time for me.

We lived in a self-imposed Jewish ghetto in the East Bronx. Although the overwhelming majority of children in my elementary school were Jewish, during December we busied ourselves with Christmas drawings and cutouts:

stockings hung over a fireplace; Christmas trees, Christmas ornaments, Christmas wreaths; Santa Claus. Our art work was hung in hallways, tacked onto bulletin boards, and taped against classroom windows. We sang *Come All Ye Faithful* and *Silent Night,* and sucked on red and white Christmas mints at Christmas parties. Children cleared out their desks and prepared for Christmas vacation. From the time I started kindergarten, until I graduated college, I could never utter the word Christmas when December came around. Instead, I substituted the words "winter recess" or "winter vacation."

Chanukah, usually celebrated around the same time as Christmas, was not the competitive holiday it is today. Jewish children lit menorah candles in the privacy of their homes. Some of them may have played with a *dredl*, some may have received Chanukah *gelt* (coins), but it wasn't a big event, like Rosh Hashanah or Pesach. There was no recognition of any Jewish holiday in our school.

In 1949, I was back in a Bronx classroom, this time as the teacher. In December, snowflake designs cut from squares of white paper decorated my second-grade classroom windows. Paintings and drawings on the walls reflected the winter season—trees laden with snow, ice-skating in Bronx Park, snowmen with carrot noses. At our "winter recess" party, complete with healthy treats like fruit, nuts, and oatmeal cookies, we played games and sang popular songs. No religious holidays were acknowledged.

Elsewhere in the school Christmas decorations were abundant. How did my Jewish colleagues feel? I wondered, but didn't ask, as we sang the traditional Christmas songs, invoking the spirit of Christmas. Both as a youngster and as a young teacher I never shared my angst about Christmas with anyone. Nor had any of my friends or colleagues confided theirs. It felt like I was a minority of one.

After moving to the suburbs in 1953, I joined the local chapter of American Jewish Congress (AJC), a political action organization whose agenda included elimination of religious holiday observances in public schools. Hallelujah! I was one of many. Since then, an increasingly diverse religious and ethnic population has prompted greater sensitivity on the subject. The First Amendment Center issues guidelines endorsed by seventeen religious and educational groups (including AJC) intended to provide direction to school boards, parents, administrators, teachers, and students on issues concerning religious holidays.

The Supreme Court is not clear regarding the limits on religious holiday celebrations in the public schools, but adheres to the First Amendment prohibition against school sponsored endorsement of religious beliefs of any kind. The high court considers a crèche—and a menorah—to be religious symbols. The majority of the justices has stated, however, that **Christmas trees** have achieved a secular status in our society and can be displayed standing alone. The First Amendment Center writes that many Americans continue to view Christmas trees as religious symbols, and for this reason schools may wish to be more sensitive than the law allows.*

For me, a Christmas tree, the single most visible symbol of Jesus' birthday, comes with emotional baggage. In the home of a Jew, it's called a "Chanukah bush," to my mind, a *shande* (shameful). And one day, I found myself staring at such a tree—in the home of a Jew—the home of my son. I felt like I'd been punched in the stomach. The floor beneath me seemed to give way.

My daughter-in-law is not Jewish. She and my son are secular people and do not practice any religion. So what was a decorated evergreen doing in a corner of their living room? They assured me that a Christmas tree is a secular symbol—without religious significance. They want their sons to know the joy of having a tree as their mother knew it in her childhood. My grandchildren enjoy the Jewish tradition of a menorah and lighting candles on the eight nights of Chanukah. With time, I came to realize that a Christmas tree is as much a part of their family history as is a menorah.

Easter, the celebration of the resurrection of Jesus Christ, not Christmas, is when pogroms against Jews have historically taken place. Easter Passion plays, produced in every language throughout the world, not Christmas trees, provide a major cause of ongoing negative attitudes towards Jews and Judaism.

There is a tendency by historians in modern times to reclaim Jesus as a Jew. Reading some of the differing accounts of his life has altered my perception of him. Albert Einstein, Sholem Asch, and Martin Buber considered him a compassionate rabbi who preached universal love. Marc Chagal painted him on the cross wearing a *tallis*, and called him a great poet and symbol of Jewish suffering. I've come to think of him as a nice Jewish boy, much like an anti-war flower child of the '60s. Little did he know what impact he would have on this world.

From time to time I've taken friends to see the spectacular "Christmas House" in my neighborhood, outlined in red and white lights, its lawn covered with whistling electric trains, life-size puppets, rampaging red-nosed reindeer, marching soldiers, a barking dog, and twinkling trees. I avoid looking at the manger scene, but standing in the crowd with all the other spectators, enveloped by the cheery strains of Jingle Bells, I don't feel threatened.

In recent times most Jewish museums across the country offer a special day of Jewish family fun on December 25th —games, arts and crafts, storytelling, and music—affirming that Jewish children need special consideration at this time. How comforting it would have been for me when I was growing up.

* First Amendment Center. firstamendmentcenter.org.

22

Identity

The 1960s and '70s were years of social and cultural protest: anti-war, civil rights, women's rights, drugs. My teenage sons challenged established attitudes toward sex and marriage, money, recreation, music, food, appearance, and religion. I was lucky; some of my friends' children followed exotic gurus, joined cults, and became members of Jews for Jesus.

During that time, in 1967, Jewish philosopher Emil Fackenheim created a "614th commandment" forbidding Jews to grant Hitler a posthumous victory, and ordering us to survive as Jews, "lest the Jewish people perish." Translation: pass along your Jewish identity. Our sons were twelve and fifteen at the time, and that's what Arthur and I thought we were doing.

My identity took root in my Jewish home during the Great Depression. My parents talked about Jewish life in the

Old Country, kept *Shabbes* as a special day, and sent me to Talmud Torah to learn Hebrew and Yiddish. We celebrated the holidays, ate matzah, potato *latkes*, and *hamantashen*. Once a month we went to *Landsleit* meetings. Most significantly, we spoke *mameloshen*—Yiddish—the mother tongue. I always knew who I was—a *Yiddishe maidel*, a Jewish girl— and then a true *Yiddishe mama*. My parents did not consciously set out to pass along Jewish identity. They were who they were.

After World War II, newly married couples tended to veer away from the religious observances and cultural expressions of their parents. I maintained a watered down version of some of the rituals ingrained in my youth, like keeping a kosher kitchen and observing the Sabbath. Because I felt so Jewish, I imagined my children would feel it too. Looking back on it, I'm not sure our sons were aware that the chopped liver, chicken noodle soup, and boiled chicken we ate on Friday nights were traditional *Shabbat* dinners. They may never have heard me mention the word *Shabbes*. Although our family did not embrace traditional *Shabbes M'tor nits*—thou shalt not write, travel, or listen to the radio—I did consider it a day apart, a day of rest, a day for fun. Saturdays were special to the boys because school was not in session and because we often went to theatre matinees.

When our older son turned ten, Arthur and I began shopping for a synagogue. It was important to us that our sons receive a liberal Jewish education, so we interviewed the rabbis and "auditioned" the cantors of all the congregations in our Queens neighborhood. We chose a Reform temple because Reform Judaism views itself as an evolving religion. The cantor's magnificent voice sealed the deal.

Our family attended holiday services and the boys learned to read Hebrew. We celebrated their Bar Mitzvahs, which were followed by two years of additional study. They did not, however, find much inspiration, joy, or spirituality in our temple. Their Jewish education did little to strengthen their bond with Judaism.

My parents had not spoken any Yiddish with me, or with one another, for more than a decade by the time their grandchildren were born. Retaining one's ethnic language was not in vogue at that time. Assimilation was the pervasive mind-set. Arthur and I sprinkled irreplaceable Yiddish words like *farblundjet* and *farmisht* into our spoken English, or used the language as code on occasion, but we never spoke it in normal conversation. Not speaking Yiddish with my sons is high on my *regret* list. *Mameloshen* was the warm and wonderful language of my youth, but it was as foreign to my boys as Chinese.

Not until the 1980s did Yiddish gain new appreciation within the Jewish community. Yiddish *vinkels* began to sprout up all over the cultural landscape. Some universities added it to their curriculum. And I came to believe that speaking the language at home would have been the optimum way to enhance my sons' Jewish identity.

Along with a renewed interest in Yiddish came the revival of klezmer and other Yiddish instrumental and vocal music. The boys missed out on the Yiddish folk songs and

Klezmer tapes we acquired after they left home. As kids they listened to our recordings of American musicals like *South Pacific* and *Man of La Mancha,* or classical selections by Copeland and Beethoven. The records they bought were mostly jazz, rock, and the new minimalist compositions. They are music lovers, and have given us gift recordings of Jewish music, but they've rarely added any to their own extensive CD collections.

My favorite piece of jewelry in those days was a pendant proclaiming "War is not healthy for children and other living things." With only a short respite in between, *war* was an ongoing occurrence. WWII, Korea, Vietnam! Young men were drafted and sent off to kill. Some were maimed for life; others never returned. Toy soldiers, tanks, and guns became common playthings; they were taboo in our house. The fairy tales and books I read to my boys were monitored for violence. So were the movies and television they watched. How sensitive, kind, and peace-loving my children turned out to be. They were both caught up in the anti-war climate of the time. One son objected when any of us stepped on an ant or swatted a fly.

Jewish identity takes many forms. My sons are caring and ethical men, practicing the Jewish value of *Tikkun Olam* (repairing the world). My-Son-the-Journalist, a talk-show host, looks for "common ground" with his disparate guests. His brother's books reveal the remarkable stories of new immigrants to our country and of people living on the fringe of mainstream American life. I see the spark of the *Pintele Yid,* the definitive Jew, in each of them.

Both sons tend always to champion the underdog, but their personal experiences with anti-Semitism are minimal, and they do not see the Jew as victim. In their youth, they heard their grandmother talk about pogroms and other injustices the Jews had endured in Europe. Their father told them about anti-Semitic slurs directed at him when he was in the army. I spoke about discrimination in college admissions and in the workplace. All of us told them about the *Six Million* and my grandfather's murder in a concentration camp. Although these events had taken place in the twentieth century, it seemed to our teenage boys that we were talking about ancient history.

"There was a disconnect," one son tells me. "We thought you were paranoid when you described someone's actions as anti-Semitic, and we were tired of hearing about it. We lived in a largely Jewish middle-class neighborhood. Many of my professors and professional contacts were Jewish. From my point of view, I grew up in a world of white and Jewish privilege." Thirty-five years later, as worldly adults, my sons are more attuned to the reality of anti-Semitism, but still believe that my fears are exaggerated.

I take pride in having passed along my Jewish values. But I'm not certain I did as well in passing along my sense of Jewish pride. *What-if I could do it all over again?* How would I accomplish Fackenheim's commandment "to survive as Jews"?

Neal Roese, a psychology professor exploring the role of *what-if* thinking, writes that "without regret, basic decision-making" is impaired. "Regret in particular," he says, "is useful for signaling to people that it's time to change their strategy."* My sons have been out of the house for thirty-five years; it's too late to alter my parenting behavior. But it's never too late to laugh at oneself. One day, reminiscing with My-Son-the-Artist, I concocted a *bubbe-meiseh* about what I should have done a long time ago:

"I'd move the family to an Orthodox community so you and your brother would not be corrupted by secular Jews, agnostics, atheists and *others*," I heard myself declaring. My son's mouth hung open.

What was this strongly secular Jew saying?

"I'd enroll you in Yeshiva, to learn Hebrew and Torah."

You, a public school advocate?

"After school you'd go to Workmen's Circle for exposure to Jewish culture and social justice."

From prayer to protest?

"I'd give up my Friday night bridge games and host open-house Shabbat dinners for your friends every week."

Who would do the dishes?

"Most importantly, Yiddish would be the primary language spoken in our home."

Farblundjet? Farmisht? What fun!

We laughed at all the contradictions I posed, recognizing that behind every spoof there's a nugget of truth.

The twenty-first century has witnessed a rebirth of orthodoxy for many Jews, more observant than my Orthodox immigrant family who came to this country a hundred years ago. Yet, the majority of Jews today are not affiliated with any branch of Judaism. My grandsons are growing up with an awareness of their Jewish lineage, but with no formal Jewish education. Their parents transmit the universal values that are at the heart of Jewish experience and all religions, but abstain from religion or ritual. They have repeatedly told us that we could expose the boys to any Jewishness we wanted. But how much can grandparents do?

An article in *The Jewish Week*, by Aaron Bisman, an NYU student, blares: "Culture Is the Connection For 21st Century Jews." Bisman resonates with me. When he heard the Hebrew prayer *Avinu Malkeinu* at a rock concert, he connected with the Jewish people around him. It made him feel "part of a unique community that shared a rich and valued tradition" beyond institutionalized Judaism. His connection is with "innovative Jewish music . . . Israeli hip hop, Yiddish punk, and Sephardic rock 'n roll." **

For Arthur and me, it's a dose of this and a dash of that: sports, books, holiday celebrations, music, movies, and food. We presented our baseball-obsessed grandsons with a card set of every known Jewish Major League baseball player from the 1870s to 2003 (142 of them), which they enthusiastically added to their card collection. When our older grandson was a freshman in high school, we bought him *The Pacific*, a book of short stories by Mark Helprin, and a Chaim Potok novel, *The Chosen*, each containing magical Jewish baseball segments. He loved both books, about Jewish boys from Brooklyn, with strong, but different religious traditions. They opened him up to a world he knew nothing about. I was surprised to learn that his English teacher had already assigned *The Chosen,* a story that would never have made it to the required reading list in my day. We then gave him its sequel, *The Promise.*

Reluctantly leaving his new baby brother at home, our grandson stomped and clapped his way through a klezmer concert at the Jewish Museum. He came with us to a Workmen's Circle *Chanukah* party and to a Reform *Simchas Torah* service, both of which he found "boring." He was intrigued by *Paper Clips,* a documentary based on a middle school project in Whitwell, Tennessee, honoring Jews killed in the Holocaust. We rented the movie *School Ties* (about a lone Jewish high school student in a Christian prep school) and viewed it with both boys. It may have been their first exposure to anti-Semitism. They sat through it without an ice-cream break, mesmerized. We bought them the video.

We dip apples into honey on *Rosh Hashanah,* sing the *dredl* song on *Chanukah,* and eat *matzah-brei* during *Pesach.* On *Purim* we grind our *groggers* whenever Haman's name is mentioned. Rousing klezmer music and Jewish folk songs fill our home when *Bubeleh* and *Shaineh Punim* come to visit. First, they head for the ping-pong table in the basement. Then, on to Grandma's kitchen: salmon *gefilte fish,* broccoli *latkes, challah* French toast, a *feinkuchel* (omelet).

The boys have absorbed the humane values of their parents. The stories and essays I've written will give them a glimpse into my world and the world of their ancestors. Their exposure to Jewish culture is sporadic and fleeting, but when you add it all up, it could be more enduring than a bagel and lox sandwich. I trust that Jewishness and a sense of peoplehood will lodge somewhere in each grandson's psyche, and evolve into his own form of Jewish identity.

* Neal Roese, Ph.D. *If Only: How to Turn Regret Into Opporttheeunity*, Broadway, 2005.
** Aaron Bisman. "Culture Is The Connection For 21st Century Jews," *The Jewish Week*, January 2, 2009.

23

Bar Mitzvah

Bar Mitzvah invitations, I spot them immediately. Their envelopes stand out from the magazines, advertisements, solicitations and bills in my mail—OVERSIZED: pale pink, lilac, deep purple, blood red, silver, gold. My presence is requested at a synagogue service, celebration to follow, aka: *disco party.* Don't forget the earplugs.

With a rare exception, the parties I've been invited to in the New Millenium are loud rock galas, acutely toxic to my generation. The gyrating thirteen-year-olds and their Gen-X or Baby Boomer parents are oblivious to the physical and emotional pain inflicted upon us by the DJ, hired under the assumption that the louder, the better. At my very last bat mitzvah blast, I sat at my assigned table all evening, unable to hear the person sitting next to me, straining to be heard. I left with a sore throat and a headache.

It would have been joyous to join the dancers on the floor; we Depression Babies still do a mean Lindy Hop. But what's the fun in dancing solo, twisting my body, ears stuffed with cotton? Dancing is when my husband twirls me around, folds me in his arms and presses his cheek to mine as we melt to the strains of *You'll Never Know*, or *A Sentimental Journey*.

"Could you play a Fox Trot or a Swing?" I asked the DJ, hoping for a Tommy Dorsey or Glen Miller oldie. "Let's ask Mama," he said, pointing to the hostess. "Continue doing what you're doing," Mama told him. Translation: It's not the Forties. The DJ looked at me and shrugged, as if to say, "I'm sorry."

Was it *Chutzpadik* for me to approach the father of an impending bat-mitzvah to ask if I could request just one old-fashioned mellow partner dance at his daughter's party? "I wouldn't count on it," he murmured.

When Jewish children reach the age of maturity (thirteen for boys, twelve for girls) they become responsible for their actions. A boy "becomes a bar mitzvah," a girl "becomes a bat mitzvah." These terms, however, are more commonly used to refer to the coming-of-age ceremony itself, and we say that someone is "having a bar or bat mitzvah" (b'nai mitzvah). In 1941 when I was thirteen years old and completing my Talmud Torah education, having a bat mitzvah was unknown. Bar mitzvah was a boy thing. At the time I accepted it without question, and I imagine most of us girls did. To this day, *Haredi* (Ultra-Orthodox) Jews reject the idea that a woman can publicly read from the Torah, and do not "have bat mitzvahs" for their girls.

"Although some people wish to be 'Bar Mitzvahed' as an expression of their faith, this has no religious significance."* It is a relatively modern innovation, not mentioned in the Talmud. In most congregations, however, it is now common practice for the celebrant to read from the Torah and Haftara, and to deliver a speech, which for many years began with "Today I am a man." Some families travel to the Western Wall or to the Masada in Israel for the occasion.

Secular Jews have discovered creative and innovative approaches to carrying out the bar or bat mitzvah. A thirteen-year-old may choose to research a major topic of inquiry, such as family history, Jewish values, or role models and heroes, which would then be presented at a ceremony. At the Workmen's Circle, a culmination of a community service project often serves as the bar mitzvah observance.

My brother's bar mitzvah in 1946 took place in the small *shul* directly across the street from our apartment in the Bronx. How handsome he looked, and how grown-up he seemed in his first suit. I *kvelled* when he chanted his Torah portion. Giving a writing implement as a gift was commonplace at that time, and I chuckled when he began his speech with "Today I am a fountain-pen," a popular gag among his friends. These days it would be more accurate to declare, "Today I am an iPod."

After the ceremony, more than fifty guests left the *shul* and crowded into our one bedroom apartment. My father raised his *kiddush* cup, said the blessing over the wine, then the *motzi*, while most of the guests stood around balancing their wine and *challah*. Six dining room chairs and a half-dozen borrowed folding chairs did not provide enough seating.

My mother and her cousins had been cooking and baking all week. The cold dairy buffet they produced included gefilte fish, horseradish, jellied pike, fish *latkes*, pickled herring, vegetable chopped liver, and a huge assortment of pastries. No doubt the guests took home enough leftover honey cake and strudel to last them an entire week.

My own sons' bar mitzvah ceremonies, some twenty years afterward, were followed by sit-down hot luncheons in the temple. For my older son's reception, we engaged a folk dance caller with a reputation for inspiring teenagers to participate in Israeli and other ethnic circle dances. He and his live band also played ballroom music for adults—Cha Cha, Rhumba, Fox Trot, Swing. A photograph album documents my aunts and uncles, along with the young folk, joining hands in a *Mizelou*. What it does not reveal is that the amplification cord was cut during the party, and that for almost an hour, while a member of the band was out looking for a replacement, the guests had nothing to do but eat and talk. Arthur and I suspected that a classical music aficionado had made his statement.

Lately, the reception following a b'nai mitzvah ceremony comes in all sizes and shapes. The disco gala seems to be the most popular. In the movie, *Keeping Up With the Steins*, one family rents a cruise ship for the occasion. A competing family contemplates renting a major league baseball stadium. The old joke about lining up for an African safari bar mitzvah bash is still circulating. The national media has reported on non-Jewish youngsters requesting a bar or bat mitzvah party for themselves after attending their Jewish friends' festivities. I'm waiting to see if it will catch on.

A bar mitzvah is a very special occasion for Jewish families. A Jewish child acknowledges his ancestry by his participation. The parents and grandparents take pride in knowing they have done their part in passing down their Jewish heritage. The thirteen year-old is energized by his rite of passage and enabled to make decisions concerning his Jewishness. I now skip the disco gala, and limit my attendance to the ceremonial event and to the customary *kiddush* luncheon following it. Who can resist the lox, sturgeon, and smoked white fish? I'm not cutting the amplification cord, just cutting out the party and bequeathing it to its rightful owners: teenagers.

* B'nai Mitzvah—Wikepedia, the free encyclopedia.

24

Coming Of Age, 2005

Letter to My Grandson on His Thirteenth Birthday

Dear Nathan,

On Passover we ask: Why is this night different from all other nights? This year I ask you Nathan: Why is this birthday different from all other birthdays? Thirteen—a milestone in the life of a child! It's the age at which every Jewish child automatically *"becomes a bar mitzvah"* and assumes the rights and responsibilities of an adult.

"Having a bar mitzvah" refers to the ceremony or celebration marking this event. Some thirteen-year-olds choose to "become a bar mitzvah" without "having a bar mitzvah." Not having a bar mitzvah does not make one less of a Jew.

"Character is a muscle," writes Marc Oppenheimer in his book *Thirteen and a Day*. "It needs to be flexed in childhood, but the real training comes at the age when you're more to blame for your choices than your parents are . . . and thirteen is the sensible age for that responsibility." But does anyone really expect you to assume the responsibilities of an adult at this age? It's the time for awareness that you are beginning your adulthood.

Coming of age does not necessarily arrive at thirteen. For Roger, in Mark Helprin's "Perfection," it may have come when he saw his parents killed, at the age of three! Although I studied Yiddish and Hebrew for four years, girls did not have bat mitzvahs in 1941. Looking back on it, although I was a trustworthy kid when my thirteenth birthday came around, I was also naïve and sheltered. My coming of age hit like a thunderbolt when I was fifteen.

It was summertime, and many of my friends were going off to sleep-away camps run by Jewish charitable organizations. I was a high school sophomore, and my parents, your great grandparents, were too proud to accept a camp scholarship based on financial need. It was time to find a job.

I had already been working for several years, baby-sitting Uncle Benny's boys and helping out in his fish store before busy holidays. But now I decided I was ready for the big leagues. I put on high heels and dress-up clothing, smeared my lips with lipstick, and went out job hunting, pretending to be eighteen, the age when working papers were no longer required. Eventually, I landed a job in a dress pattern factory. Standing on my feet all day, hunched over long rows of wooden rods, I plucked off thousands of tissue paper templates and folded them into hundreds of cardboard packages, to be sold to dressmakers the world over. Boring. Exhausting.

I could barely make it home. My mother prepared my favorite desserts as a pick-me-up: apple pie, nut cake, and butter cookies. But all I wanted to do was collapse into bed. My back ached, my feet hurt, my head pounded. That's when I woke up. People were needed to grow the wheat, milk the cows, churn the butter, and gather the eggs that went into her delicious pastries. The entire economic process—from farming, to harvesting, to transportation, and to sales, which I'd always taken for granted—entered my consciousness.

Neither had I ever fully appreciated my mother's job as a homemaker: scrubbing clothes on her metal washboard, hanging them to dry in the sun, then ironing and folding them; shopping for food, boiling, broiling, and baking; scouring floors and washing dishes. For the first few years of my life we didn't own a refrigerator. Public washing machines came along much later. There were no toaster ovens or dishwashers. How did she do it? Each day I gained more and more respect for her. That was my coming of age.

For thirteen years I have watched you grow, becoming the young man you are today—at your coming of age. It is with joy and admiration that I observe the important life-style choices you are making:

Although you seemed disappointed and downcast after you chose to transfer to middle school, you made a conscious decision to stick with it. With patience you ultimately overcame the obstacles, adjusted to your new environment, and made new friends.

You were ambivalent about attending a summer school music program, which meant giving up your favorite pastime—sports. Instead of sulking, you searched for an evening baseball league, which allowed you to do both! How resourceful.

You create challenges and goals for yourself, like selecting a difficult piano concerto and teaching yourself to play it.

With practice and determination you have become a skillful athlete.

In pursuing your passion for reading, you are traveling the world without ever leaving home.

You're devoted to your brother. How lucky he is to have you as a role model.

Most of all, I love to watch you curl up with your mom or with your dad, just like you did when you were a toddler.

I was proud of your dad at his Bar Mitzvah, faultlessly reading his Torah portion, and playing his flute at the luncheon afterwards. I was proud of him when he graduated from college eight years later. Both were significant coming-of-age events. And how proud I am as I watch you mature, heading into adulthood with a growing list of outstanding character traits, having already achieved so much at this milestone birthday—thirteen.

Luvya,

Grandma

25

Unaffiliated

Synagogue affiliation: Orthodox, Conservative, Reform, or Reconstructionist, with variations in between. There were so many options open to me, but was there a branch of Judaism I could call *home*?

1972 was the year my thirty-nine-year-old brother died. He was wise and handsome, my best friend. I miss him still. His wife Barbara was comforted by going off to synagogue, but during the ten years of my affiliation with a Reform temple I had never experienced anything spiritual. Maybe this was the time for me to discover what so many others seemed to have found.

It wasn't. Going to temple offered me little consolation. I could not join the congregation in responsive reading or in reciting *kaddish* (prayer for the dead); every page sang the praises of an Almighty God. They held no meaning for me. I could not connect an Almighty God with the untimely death of this wonderful young man.

It was also the year that Arthur lost his engineering job and was filling in as substitute math teacher in a local high school. Our children had completed their religious education by that time, and we decided not to renew our temple membership for the upcoming year. I wrote a letter to our rabbi informing him of our revised financial status and expressing my hope of rejoining in the future. There was no response to my letter. Disappointed, we never returned, never rejoined.

My attendance at the temple had been limited, a "Holiday Jew" you could call me. The fall holiday of *Rosh Hashanah* inaugurates a ten-day period for personal introspection: recognizing that we have the ability to change, to break old habits, to say "I'm sorry," and to work towards being a better person. I had always marveled that such a holiday exists and I missed the communal experience. I saw people coming from synagogue dressed in holiday finery and I felt like an orphan. Although I was not inspired when I belonged to a temple, as an unaffiliated Jew, I felt afloat, and guilty about not supporting a Jewish house of worship.

Now that *we* were "at liberty," friends and relatives began inviting us to their congregations for the High Holidays. As a married person, the word WE was prominent in my vocabulary: *we* went to the movies, *we* traveled, *we* danced. *We* were bridge partners—that was the riskiest WE; *we* went to temple on Rosh Hashanah—the most halfhearted WE. I was more than pleased to be observing the holiday with my friends; Arthur could have done without the services. But he was flexible and went along with whatever I decided to do.

Like dine-around club members, we found ourselves sampling a variety of services, initially, all of them **Reform**. The Long Island temple we first attended was smaller and more progressive than the one we had belonged to in Queens. I was thrilled to see a woman rabbi officiating. Twenty-five years later I participated in a service at the 92nd Street Y. Encountering a woman rabbi had become a routine occurrence by then; still, I *kvelled* at her lively and humorous sermon. The congregation we visited in New Jersey seemed younger, more ethnically diverse, and more ritually observant than the others. A cluster of men were *davening* (praying) up at the *bima*, and I could not determine which one was the rabbi.

Each year, on *Yom Kippur*, Arthur and I went to a nearby temple for *yizkor*, a memorial service open to the community. Afterwards, non-members were invited to the temple's serene and elegant main sanctuary for the concluding service and *shofar* blowing. The professional choir and magnificent stained glass windows added to the significance of the occasion. *Wherever I went, I found myself searching for segments in the prayer book that were relevant and meaningful to me personally, instead of reciting the passages in praise of God.*

I once accompanied my mother to a *Rosh Hashanah* service in her senior residence, where Young Israel, an

Orthodox sect, set up a makeshift synagogue each year. Not knowing how to read Hebrew, Arthur drew the line at flexibility and did not join us. Ma introduced me to her friends and stroked my arm repeatedly, happy to have me sitting next to her; I was happy to be there with her. The contrast between the Reform services I was accustomed to and this Orthodox service was stark. The women were separated from the men by a large white sheet; I never got to see the rabbi, or the *bima*. No English was spoken; there was no responsive reading. I joined the congregation in reading the Hebrew passages from the *siddur* and was surprised to find that not understanding what I was reciting was helpful. I was not bothered by praise-God passages. Instead, the repetition of meaningless Hebrew syllables had the same effect as the Hindu mantra I used for meditation. They were restful and calming.

From time to time I attended my sister-in-law's **Conservative** *shul*, to listen to her husband, the cantor. Despite the long service, I enjoyed his beautiful baritone rendition of the traditional prayers. A good cantor enriches my synagogue experiences, turning them into musical events. Venturing into a neighborhood Conservative synagogue, I was delighted by the preponderance of music included in the service and the spirited singing of the congregants. Nowadays, I look forward to a relaxation "fix" at yet another nearby Conservative *shul*, where an Israeli cantor, accompanied by guitar and accordion, conducts monthly *Ahava* (love) meditation fests.

I am happy to be connected to a Jewish environment, with my people, in whatever synagogue or temple I find myself. Yet, I feel detached from the ritual itself. Recent studies show that less than 50 percent of Jews in the United States are affiliated with organized religion. My guess is that many of them, like me, find the liturgy off-putting. Synagogue affiliation does not define me as a Jew. My Jewishness is inseparable from who I am.

"Dine-around" had not brought me any closer to finding a "home." Never having been to a **Reconstructionist** service, I tried to locate a group practicing in Queens, but there was none. So when a friend invited us to a *Purim* celebration in his synagogue on Long Island, I quickly accepted. It was a festive event; I enjoyed it. Reconstructionist Judaism believes in "the human authorship of all religious traditions as opposed to the traditional Jewish view that God's command is what makes rituals mandatory." *Human authorship of religious traditions*—I liked that—but I knew very little about the language of their liturgy. Had there been a congregation closer to home, I would have sampled a routine *Shabbat* service. Reconstructionism might have proven to be a good fit.

Starting in the late 1990s, Arthur and I took Jewish literature courses at a learning center for retired teachers. The curriculum ranged from the Torah to *Pirkei Avot* (Ethics of our Fathers) to Chaim Grade, a secularized Yiddish author and poet. Our learned instructor had studied for the rabbinate as a young man, and in private conversation informed us about **Humanistic Judaism**, a "fifth branch" of Judaism. Established by Rabbi Sherwin T. Wine in the mid-1960s in suburban Detroit, the Society for Humanistic Judaism (SHJ) offers a non-theistic alternative in contemporary Jewish life, providing a home for humanistic, secular, and cultural Jews. It includes celebrating Jewish holidays and life-cycle events with meaning and relevance to our time. I was not surprised to learn that my Jewish literature teacher was the *madrikh* (leader) of the local chapter for Humanistic Judaism.

With our instructor at the helm, and a "program" in our hands, Arthur and I began attending Humanistic *Rosh Hashanah* celebrations, not services in the traditional sense. The candle lighting ceremony proclaimed our link to the past and to our heritage. The readings recognized Rosh Hashanah as a turning point, weaving together the past and the present. For the first time I understood the blast of the *shofar* to be a wake-up call. I was totally immersed in the proceedings: remembering loved ones and those who perished in acts of war and terrorism, reciting a secular *Shema*, affirming responsibilities to the world community, and singing contemporary folksongs along with familiar Hebrew melodies. I did not need to search for meaningful passages in a prayer book. It was all meaningful.

In 2003, Sherwin Wine came to New York. His lucid lecture on Secular Humanistic Judaism articulated my own beliefs: A Jew is someone who identifies with the history, culture, struggles, triumphs, and survival of the Jewish people; we are a family. Rabbi Wine and I were in perfect harmony. I felt privileged to be in the audience, but sorry I hadn't invited all my friends to join me. My presence at Humanist meetings, however, continued to be sporadic.

In the spring of 2007, Arthur and I attended a lively discussion on the Ten Commandments and its relevance to society today. Alas, it turned out to be the last session of a Saturday afternoon Modern Jewish History series. I was sorry to learn that my former instructor, the *madrikh*, had passed away. His dedicated protégé had taken over the role, and the group was renamed the Queens Community for Cultural Judaism (QCCJ). Although the modern history series was completed, we returned for the next meeting, featuring a talk on the *Jewish daily Forward*, by Michael Baron, a Yiddishist. He interspersed his dynamic presentation with Yiddish *leedl* (folk songs), and I was in Yiddish heaven. At a subsequent meeting we took a look at the Torah and the differing versions of *Creation*. Three glorious, invigorating *Shabbes* afternoons—I was ready for more.

My first *Yom Kippur* meeting with the QCCJ consisted of material from diverse sources such as the Bible, Reform Judaism, Beethoven, Debbie Friedman, and John Lennon. The program included a rendition of *Kol Nidre* with cello and clarinet; the Yiddish, Hebrew, and English songs were performed by the group's vice president, a spirited guitar-strumming folksinger. Its new *madrikh*, a professional clarinetist, concluded the holiday event with the traditional blowing of the *shofar*, transferring our meeting room, in the basement of the Unitarian Universalist Congregation, into a sacred place and a concert hall. What a mean *shofar* that man blows.

I look forward to the upcoming sessions on Jewish literature and to celebrating Jewish holidays in a community of like-minded folks. So does Arthur; he's not just tagging along. *We* have found a home—not only for the High Holidays.

RETIREMENT 1984

26

What Do You Do All Day?

Twice a year Winnie hopped the bus from New Jersey, while I boarded the Long Island Railroad for our traditional birthday get-togethers in Manhattan. Munching on lettuce leaves, we had each altered our diets. Our conversation, however, had not changed since my retirement in 1984. We chatted about old friends, our aging parents, and teacher burn-out. Once again, Winnie divulged her fears about retiring and repeated the question that had also become a tradition, *"What do you do all day?"*

Winnie was not alone. At parties, a chance encounter, wherever I went, I was asked the same questions: What do you do with yourself now that you're retired? Aren't you bored? Don't you miss the structure of a job? How do you fulfill your need for accomplishment? The same work ethic we Depression Babies had all inherited.

In 1936, when my family moved to a new neighborhood, meeting Winnie in third grade opened my eyes. My home was quiet, somber, a place to toil. All day my mother scrubbed, ironed, cooked, and baked with furrowed brow. In my friend's home, up the hill and around the corner, I found an aura of levity. Winnie's mother, curled up on the couch, read a book, or chatted on the telephone. Every week she and her "girls" gathered for lunch and to play mah-jongg. I watched their fingers fly over the exotic colored tiles, and when they departed, my girls and I, thrilled by the touch of ivory, would play until sundown. On Saturday nights Winnie's parents dressed up and went out to the movies.

Down the hill my mother was shredding, slicing, sautèing, and kneading, preparing bundles of her famous gefilte fish and cheese blintzes for her aging mother, her ailing cousin, and her pregnant sister. She played no games, she didn't make time to read a book, and on Saturday nights she baked her celebrated cakes, cookies, and *ruggelach* for the *mishpocheh* coming to visit on Sunday. While I was ogling Winnie's mother, was she ogling mine?

Like my mother, Winnie and I are rooted in the depression, in toil. We had outdone our mothers—balancing home, family, and career while squeezing in some up-the-hill levity on weekends. My friend wanted to retire from her job as an early childhood teacher, but envisioning Skid Row, rocking chairs, and TV soaps was fearful of taking that awesome step. Our children did not share our heritage, leaving us behind in the dust of their own liberated footprints through life. It was the time for reflection and reevalutaion. What did we want to do with the rest of our lives?

A sabbatical year of discovery disproved the notion that the human race is faced with a cruel choice: work or day-time television. I found a diverse and challenging world awaiting me outside my fifth-grade classroom. A year later, I gave myself the gift of a permanent sabbatical. Retirement was graduation—ending one important chapter in my life, moving on to another, new and more wonderful.

"Winnie," I told her, "it's not so much what I do, but my altered state of being." In the liberty of retirement I am free to have insomnia without anxiety, to take a midmorn-ing walk, an extended weekend out-of-town, an off-season vacation. I'm free to stay indoors and gaze in wonderment at the snowflakes gently blanketing the streets instead of worrying about driving conditions. If I'm reading a book I can't put down, I don't. I put the world on hold while I have a love affair with my favorite author. I am a caterpiller, turned into a butterfly.

What do I *do* all day? Lunch at the White House? Rendezvous with an old boyfriend? I mold fantasy and real-ity into a nugget of graduation goals, the foundation of that trip into space beyond the classroom. Most significantly, my up-the-hill fun activities are no longer squeezed in or re-served for weekends; they are now relegated to prime time. I am responsible only for myself, and after a lifetime of few options I am able to make choices of how to spend each precious moment.

My mom was in her mid-eighties, and living in a senior residence when I retired. I visited her daily, delivering bags of food from the supermarket and the kosher butcher. Stella D'Oro cookies had replaced her home-baked pastries, but she continued to cook her other renowned specialties for friends and family. She could not fathom my early retirement, and she too asked the question, *"What do you do all day?"*

There are not enough hours in the day. I play bridge, I square dance, I go antiquing, I read a lot. But there's more, much more. I was overjoyed when I spotted a listing for a seminar: Women and Wellness. I asked a friend to join me; the incredulous expression on her face was her response. I cajoled my bridge partner into attending a course on women in the Bible. Was she in the wrong pew! I joined a Gurdjieff study group, based on the principle of changing negative inclinations, the *yetzer hara*. Several friends accompanied me to a session. Only one returned. My "postgraduate" regimen is relevant only to me. My friends' choices will be uniquely their own.

"What do you do?" a stranger at a party asked me, referring to job function. I hesitated. How should I answer? I was a teacher? Or, I'm retired? What am I? Who am I? Have I been diminished by retirement? Winnie and I are the insecure children of the depression, fearful of the economics of retirement. But the question exposed our major fear—loss of identity. Most fears are irrational and this proved to be no exception.

Three years after I retired, I was diagnosed with uterine cancer and required a hysterectomy. My surgeon severed an artery during the procedure, but neglected to tell me about it. For many months I was unable to sit up or walk without assistance. It was the most frightening time of my life. Finally, another surgeon identified the problem. I was furious! Why hadn't I been told? So much anxiety could have been avoided. I wanted to publish an article, to make my experience public, but didn't know where to begin.

A course at the New School on writing the personal essay helped me record my story. To my surprise, something wondrous emerged from my effort. All the urgency, anger, and frustration had evaporated, the incident relegated to history. From the melange of my many activities, writing superceded them all, and escalated into a passion, wonderful and all consuming. Flashing memories, innovative wording, structural changes, and future story topics are always running through my head. They interfere with my bidding at the bridge table, usurp the speaker at a lecture, blot out the caller at the other end of the phone line, and keep me awake at night. Writing has not only enriched my life, the intense focus has given me a new identity—an identity beyond job function. Look Ma, I'm a writer.

Old passions are waiting to be awakened, new passions to be discovered. My comrades-in-retirement developed a passion for growing exotic bromeliaceae, singing in a chorus, and fabricating stained glass lampshades. They graduated to acquiring tennis trophies, mediating civil disputes, and rediscovering the joys of Yiddish. They found structure as docents lecturing in art museums, and assuaged their need for accomplishment teaching English to Russian immigrants. Many of them became political activists. My friend Sylvia's doodling in the margins of her notebook has evolved into colorful collages, adorable dolls, exquisite pins and pendants. Perhaps, like my friend Ben, Winnie's passion would be aroused onstage, as a supernumerary at the Metropolitan Opera.

In 1990, Winnie gave herself the gift of retirement. During the first four years away from her classroom she took courses at Elderhostel, accompanied her daughter on business trips, drove to Yellowstone National Park, and spent hours each week playing with her grandchildren. She was learning to play bridge; we discussed bidding techniques and play-of-the-hand strategies. She joined a square dance club; we planned on linking arms at a dance convention.

Winnie and I met for lunch to celebrate her 66th birthday. "*So, what do you do all day?*" I asked, biting into a veggie burger. "*So, why didn't I retire sooner?*" she grinned, sprinkling honey mustard dressing onto her salad. Living up the hill is most certainly not over the hill.*

Postscript:

Four months later, on July 4th, while she was driving to meet a friend for dinner, a car going the wrong way smashed into Winnie's Ford. That driver was unhurt, but my beloved Winnie was killed instantly. I miss her. I miss our birthday get-togethers. I miss reminiscing about the good old days and hearing about the good new days. She earned my magna cum laude retirement award for awakening old passions and discovering new ones.

* Ruth Lehrer. Adapted from "No Job With Benefits" by Ruth Lehrer, *Hadassah Magazine*, November 1992.

27

On Being Grandma

1991: I Am Not A Grandma

In my bridge group, I am the only one. Of my House Plan sisters, I am the only one. In my old neighborhood crowd, I am the only one—who is not a grandma.

"You don't have children? What do you do for aggravation?" The bittersweet joke circulated among us mommies when the kids were growing up.

"You're not a grandma?" half question, half expression of sympathy from grandmas I encounter everywhere. "What sort of pleasure have you," the question seems to imply, "without a cute and cuddly presence in your life?"

My sons, both married and approaching their forties, have cast me in a new role—a member of a transient minority and a diminishing support group. I am no longer one of the "girls." My friend Kate became a grandma twenty years ago, at age forty-three. She was the first. Since then, my other friends have slowly joined her—one by one. For them, Toys-R-Us has upstaged Bloomies, and spending time with a grandchild receives top priority. I call a friend to join me at a library lecture, but she's going to her grandson's school play. "He's got the lead role." I never heard of a grandchild who didn't.

Almost four decades ago, my friends and I huddled together around the sandbox, and by unspoken agreement rarely discussed the children. Yet, when we meet for lunch today, "my grandson, the doctor" stories are the norm. "In your life," they begin, "you have never seen such brilliance, such sensitivity, such a sense of humor . . ."

I don't recall any of us, as parents, passing around photos. Whipping out the latest baby pictures, however, has now become ritual. I grin adoringly at the camera's subject, and most importantly, at the subject's grandma. Mother Nature painted each of their grandchildren beautiful and unique. Then why do all baby pictures look alike to me?

"Don't worry," these super-grandmas assure me, "one day it'll happen." The presumption is that life without grandchildren can be nothing but barren and joyless. Ironically, for me, having grandchildren could be bad for my health. There are so many things to worry about.

When I was ten years old, my friends and I walked through Crotona Park and Bronx Park, day or night. We rode the subways when we were eleven. We believed that the friendly man who spoke to us was just that—a friendly man.

He may still be so today, but with good reason we warn our children not to talk to strangers. My parents knew that parks were safe, subways were safe, schools were safe. They worried about polio, mastoids, and measles. Violence was not in their consciousness, or mine. Television did not offer it up for dessert all day; there was no television. The drugs we heard about were aspirin and argyrole. We didn't know anyone who was injured in an automobile accident; hardly anyone in the neighborhood owned a car. The streets were for playing.

Things were pretty tame in the 1950s when my sons were born. I cautioned them against playing with matches or running with scissors, and Doctor Spock was there for major emergencies. Then, in the late '60s and '70s, when my boys were finishing high school and away at college, my secure little world exploded.

For a decade, the Vietnam War hung over the nation like a vampire, sucking the blood from tens of thousands of our young men and their families. My neighbor's son escaped by running off to Canada. Others weren't so lucky. I held my breath when my sons' draft lottery numbers were issued. Perhaps their participation in loud but peaceful protest demonstrations helped to end a misguided war before they were old enough to be drafted.

That wasn't a great time to be a parent—or a grand-mother. A friend's son, away in college and high on drugs, fell off an icy bridge and drowned. Several overdosed. Psychedelic drugs blew the mind of a graduate student I knew. Twenty years later he spends his days vegetating in his parents' attic. An eighteen-year-old, who spent many hours playing ping-pong in my basement, was killed in an auto accident on school break. Too many bright young men died of AIDS. One boy I knew shaved his head and got involved in a religious cult. Another succumbed to Jews for Jesus and eventually became a Messianic minister.

I do not miss having grandchildren. I am retired from teaching, and my sons and I are "letting go," freeing ourselves from the chains that bound us. My world is populated with adults, and I love it. I am not troubled by chicken pox or broken noses. I do not baby-sit, and my home is not cluttered with portable cribs and Ninja Turtles. I am responsible to and for myself only. I have moved upward and onward, my days bursting with many passions—comfortable with my minority status and this indulgent pause in my life.

Some Grandmas proclaim that they have been given "another chance" to right the wrongs they made as young parents. Ah, that I understand. There are so many "I should haves" in the recesses of my being, that another chance in my maturity, to repeat the parenting process with my own children would be welcome; another chance to do things differently, to laugh at their long hair and scraggly beards, to relinquish my need for control. But this obviously is not possible. Neither is it the role I would play as a grandma.

No, I am not a grandma. Of course the choice is not mine. But had I joined that majority, would I be comfortable knowing that my grandchildren face a world of crumbling values, violence, drugs, pollution, and AIDS. I do not reveal these thoughts to my grandma friends. "Sour grapes," they'd think. When, on occasion, I stumble upon another non-grandma, she does not share my sentiment, and lusts for that G-word—GRANDMA. I appear to be a minority of one.

1999: Postscript

I Am Not A Grandma was written for a women's writing class in an adult education program at Queens College in the autumn of 1991. I thought it was honest, provocative, and funny. Confidently, I read it to the group. "Sour grapes," the women clamored. I had expected my grandma friends to react that way, but these were writers, critiquing a creative and candid expression of feelings. I was unprepared for the onslaught that followed. They would have stoned me if they could. A writer needs to anticipate her audience. I did not.

A few months later, My-Son-the-Journalist called. "Mom, you know that essay you wrote for your writing class? Well, get it published quickly." My stomach did a flip-flop. In the spring of 1992, *I Am Not A Grandma* appeared in *Cue*, a Queens College literary magazine. In September of that year, the cutest, sweetest, smartest little baby boy provided me with access to the much heralded G-word. I was approaching my sixty-fifth birthday. With unbridled joy I cradled my grandson in my arms. Nathan, my *Bubeleh*.

Still, I knew my "Jewish Mother Syndrome" would re-emerge. My anxiety began the day of his birth. Certain he'd contract an upper respiratory infection, I watched as he was passed from one visitor to another, everyone's teddy bear. When I discovered that his "crib" was the family bed, I worried that he'd be smothered in his sleep. At other times I pictured him crawling out to the terrace of his eighteenth-floor apartment. Worry turned to fear when my grandchild was rushed to the hospital with an asthmatic attack or severe allergic reaction.

When *Bubeleh* was two years old, Grandpa and I started a weekly ritual—driving into Manhattan to pick him up for a day on-the-town. "Ready to go," he'd proclaim, climbing into his stroller as soon as he saw us enter the apartment. We'd scoop up our prize and head out—to the Staten Island Ferry, a percussion group at Damrosch Park, a magic performance, a miniature train exhibit. Outings with Nathan became the highlight of my retirement.

One heavily trafficked Sunday afternoon, when Nathan was six, we dashed into his apartment, late for a Klezmer concert at the Jewish Museum, and returned to the car with a crying, growling child, clutching his baseball cap. "I don't want to go to a concert, I don't want to go anywhere. I have too many activities. I want to stay home and play with my toys," he shouted. What he did not say, what he most likely didn't realize, was that he'd be leaving his new baby brother Simon (*Shaineh Punim*) alone with his parents.

So Grandpa and I relinquished our job as tour guides and became Nathan's play-date companions. We'd stretch out on his living room rug, while he pulled out Monopoly, checkers, and a deck of cards. We'd watch his favorite baseball video, *Little Big League;* innings—not outings. Nathan was not the only one happy to be there, stretched out on the carpet—relaxed, at home plate.

2002: Epilogue

"Grandma, Grandpa, will you play with me?" my younger grandson asks, spilling his Tinkertoy or Thomas train set onto the carpet as we walk through the door. *Shaineh Punim* has never been "ready to go." We've taken him to the playground, but we've never gone out on-the-town. I recall our wonderful outings with Nathan, and I think perhaps we're shortchanging this youngster. But then I see him playing, engrossed and so content. A child's work, after all, is to play. I wonder now, were the days we spent running around with Nathan for his benefit or for ours?

2009: Addendum

"I should have skipped the children and gone straight to the grandchildren," grandmas everywhere tell me. As Grandma, I'm not the one that "sets limits" or issues "time-out" directives to my grandsons. Nor do I nag them to clean their rooms or to practice the piano. My relationship with them is one of pure fun and love. But once again, this is not a great time to be a parent—or a grandparent.

Almost seventeen, Nathan has emerged from his childhood world of computer games and Little League. News reports on TV and computer blogs disturb him: street crime, campus shootings, religious hatred, suicide bombings. The world he knows is peaceful and loving, a powerful pitch on the baseball field the most aggressive act he has performed. Why do people hate each other? Or kill each other? The adults in his life ask the very same questions.

I wish I could offer my grandchildren a world without war, terror, massive debt, pollution, or religious fanaticism—a world with medical cures from stem cell research and voting machines without erectile dysfunction. Nathan will be eighteen in a year. Will the government enact a military draft and send him off to kill, or to be killed? I shudder at the thought. There's so much to worry about. Still, the joy factor continues to multiply. *Bubeleh* and *Shaineh Punim* are coming for a sleep-over this weekend. Grandpa and I are teaching them to play bridge. Next week we're going to Simon's school play. He's got the lead role—of course.

28

The Work

"Who's that?" I asked, twenty years ago, when my friend Ann invited me to her weekly *Gurdjieff* study group. His name has been a household word in my family ever since.

An early twentieth century Armenian philosopher, George I. Gurdjieff taught a system of living with *intense consciousness* called *The Work*. Study groups are held in various countries around the world. The leader of Ann's Long Island section was a slim, gentle seventy-five-year-old Orthodox Jewish woman, whom I shall call Sophie. An observant Jew, studying and teaching the work of a religious Catholic, she added a unique Jewish perspective, sprinkling her lectures with numerous references to Torah and to God.

The group members were mostly non-observant Jewish women, ranging in age from fifty to eighty. They functioned as a support group, helping each other with troubling personal issues. I bonded with them almost immediately, and for the next eight years I didn't miss a session.

Studying Gurdjieff is a life's work, and includes learning a new vocabulary. The word *"struggle"* (fight against negativity) is pervasive in *The Work*. Coincidentally, or perhaps indicative of the times, all eight of us were *struggling* with similar issues that summer of 1988: health, intermarriage, misunderstandings, the generation gap, and driving with a spouse. Going for a second helping of strawberry shortcake or an extra slice of pizza was a weighty issue for some of the women. The "Jewish Mother Syndrome," behavior I learned from my mother, which she learned from hers, was a major concern for me.

Jewish Mother jokes—a sure-fire winner in a comedian's arsenal—are stereotypical and exaggerated. But for me, they contain more than a nugget of truth.

"What did Einstein's Jewish mother say when he won the Nobel Prize?"

"Before they come to photograph you, do something with your hair."

I would have given Einstein the same advice. I'm a worrier, overprotective, controlling, and fearful. Having negative thoughts, or "negative awareness," is not being *conscious*. Sophie and the other women in the group helped me to identify and address my destructive behavior patterns (*yetzer hara*). Transforming negative reactions into positive ones was the next step. Handling a situation wisely won't happen in a negative state.

Together we women read and discussed passages in the written works of G.I. Gurdjieff (*Meetings with Remarkable Men*), P.D. Ouspensky (*The Fourth Way, In Search of the Miraculous*), and Maurice Nicoll (*Commentaries on The Teaching of Gurdjieff and Ouspensky*). Essentially, the readings focused on aspects of *consciousness*, being aware of one's self, even when doing mechanical things—or as we say in *The Work*—*awakening from sleep*.

Weekly assignments, focusing our attention on every-day tasks, were an integral part of our study. We observed ourselves speaking on the phone, preparing dinner, eating, doing the dishes, going for a walk. I became aware that I ate too quickly, spoke too loudly, clenched my jaw, did not always remember if I had taken my vitamins. When any negative situation occurred, I reviewed the *chatter* (internal negative dialogue) in my mind, observed my anger and frustration, paid attention to what my body was doing, and attempted to relax the tension. In class we reserved time for group meditation and *sensing* (focusing our awareness on our body parts). Finally, I confronted the *illusion* that I was *conscious*. Most of the time we operate out of *mechanicality*. *Waking-up* is a *struggle*. Prospective group members came and went, choosing not to *struggle*, preferring to *sleep*.

Sophie encouraged personal consultations. I valued her opinions and treasured my private time with her. *Standing in their shoes,* one of her favored strategies, helped me become *less judgmental and accepting of both friends and family members and their lifestyle choices.* I might have allowed Einstein to wear his hair any way he desired! How I wished I could go back in time and try out the lessons I learned from *The Work*. My sons watched as their Jewish Mother gradually "let go." They called me their "Gurdjieffian Mom."

I considered Sophie my Guru. Together we had accomplished so much. Then, on the day after Baruch Goldstein, an Israeli fundamentalist, massacred twenty-nine Muslims praying in the Cave of the Patriarchs, the image of my guru was shattered. While millions of Jews around the world were aghast at his action, my friend and mentor condoned it. "He is giving us a wake-up call," she told the group. Perhaps he was, but was slaughtering human beings the way to do this? Instantly, the passages Sophie had so often touted came to mind: *"Everything based on violence can only create violence." "There is not a single school of real teaching that teaches violence."* Was Sophie doing *The Work*?

The other group members, who all agreed with me, shrugged their shoulders and overlooked her outrageous comment, just as we had all overlooked her abundant references to God in the past. We excerpted what was relevant to ourselves, focusing on our goals for personal transformation, not on the religious or political attitudes of our teacher. But Sophie's viewpoint on the slaughter was unacceptable to me. I felt betrayed, and quit the group. Was I doing *The Work*?

Three years later I returned, determined not to be put off by political issues. The self-awareness and insight I had gained during those eight years of study was fading, and I missed what had become an integral part of my life. During my absence Sophie had become even more religious. She welcomed me warmly, and I was glad to be back. Later that year, in a conversation about the Gaza and West Bank settlements, I was not too surprised when she defended the settlers' right to be there.

"God gave us that land; it's written in the Bible," she declared. "We cannot give up one inch of it, and if necessary we'll hold on to it by force." The Bible? By force? I could not stand by and shrug my shoulders. Once again Sophie and I were not of like mind. From her Orthodox viewpoint: "He, who maintains that the Torah is not divinely revealed, is an *apikores*" (heretic). I was already reconciled to that difference between us. But again, faced with the issue of force, I hearkened back to *The Work*: "Everything based on violence can only create violence." Sophie informed me of our "irreconcilable differences," and I was compelled to leave the group yet again.

Since then, I've reviewed the voluminous notes I took during our sessions and read passages from some of the books I had acquired. My friend Ann is the only group member still available to speak with, and we occasionally lapse into Gurdjieffian jargon. Without the reinforcement and support of the group and its leader, however, I am not always successful in applying *The Work* to my negative reactions. Politics aside, Sophie helped me to "wake up," and to "let go." My sons and I shall always be grateful.

29

Vacationing With Elderhostel

Arthur and I (born two days apart) couldn't wait for our sixtieth birthdays. Some of our older friends were feasting on a smorgasbord of Elderhostel seminars affiliated with educational institutions in the USA and abroad. Not until the winter of 1988 were we finally eligible to join them. Hallelujah!

To escape New York's frigid weather, we chose a jazz and history program at Southeastern Louisiana University, forty miles from New Orleans. An old dormitory, vacant for three years, had been reopened for our group. The walls and ceiling of our room were peeling. The semi-private accommodations we'd been told about translated into toilets and showers down a long dark corridor. The odor of cleansers was pervasive. Fortunately, I squelched the urge to flee.

The instructors were excellent, the courses absorbing. But the spirit and savvy of the Elderhostelers, some of them well into their eighties, was even more impressive. Dining on po-boys and pizza, we mingled with the undergraduates in the school cafeteria, a nostalgic reminder of days long past. When the temperature plunged suddenly and snow fell during lunch one day, the young students cheered wildly, never having seen soft white flakes descending from the sky. Although the snowfall was light, the school shut down and with it, the cafeteria. So much for the sunny south. Local residents remained indoors, and we seniors, mostly from the north, were alone on the icy road that night, in search of a meal. Out of nowhere, a pair of huge white marble lion sculptures appeared in the darkness, welcoming us to the most palatial Chinese restaurant any of us had ever seen. The food was almost as impressive as the décor.

Each evening, reluctant to return to our aromatic digs, a large group of us gathered in the lobby past midnight, exchanging stories and jokes. By week's end, we'd become old friends, planning a mini-reunion for the spring—the first of many reunions yet to come, with new friends we were yet to meet. Arthur and I were hooked. Since then we've taken most of our vacations with Elderhostel, discussing Pat Conroy in Georgia, learning to play the dulcimer in Maine, exploring the galleries at the Art Institute in Chicago.

Most especially, I enjoy going to Elderhostels in the south, where Jews had a significant presence even before the American Revolution. We had chosen our first program because of its proximity to New Orleans, and we spent time touring that grand old city, ogling its ornate filigreed wrought iron balconies and looking for signs of Jewish life.

We sought out Touro Synagogue and Temple Sinai; both were closed. The Ranger tours we took included information about the city's diverse ethnic population, but had not provided a clue about Jews living or studying there. Years later, Elderhostel instituted a Jewish New Orleans program, which turned out to be one of its most popular offerings before Katrina. I'm hoping it will be revived in the future.

Driving home one winter, we spent some time in Savannah, Georgia, where we attended a *Shabbes* service in Temple Mickve Israel. A startling gothic structure, it is located in one of the city's twenty-one squares, landscaped with live oaks, azaleas, fountains, and statues. Founded in 1733, it houses a museum with an impressive collection of Jewish memorabilia, most prominently, a letter to the congregation from George Washington. The rabbi, alert to newcomers in the sanctuary, invited us to the *Oneg Shabbat*, and directed his congregants to welcome us. Southern hospitality is not a myth. Those people made me feel like a lost relative visiting from out-of-town.

The following year we returned to Mickve Israel for an Elderhostel on the Jews of China. There are Jews in China? I was fascinated by the rabbi's tale of Jewish traders in the early eighth century who traveled the Silk Road, settled in Kaifeng (a city south of Beijing), married Chinese women, and practiced Jewish rituals for some 800 or more years. Sisterhood provided our meals, all of it southern fare and too spicy for me. Chinese food would have been a nice touch.

We found no Jewish history, but a lot of Jewish participants, in Jekyll Island, about seventy miles south of Savannah. For three consecutive years we sampled their courses on parent-child relationships in Shakespeare, the Barrier Islands, laughter, magic, antiques, and southern writers. During a lecture on Carson McCullers, an Elderhosteler raised his hand. "Why are there so many Jews at this Elderhostel?" he asked. A startled hush settled over the classroom. The Jewish instructor waited a minute or two before replying. "What do *you* think?" he asked. Quickly the man responded, "Because Jews have money." People around me gasped, and the questioner's wife turned ghostly white. I felt her pain. "Don't get me wrong," the man growled, "I don't have an anti-Semitic bone in my body." After a long pause, he added, "Except one." He then proceeded to explain that he had worked on a missile program with a brilliant German scientist, who was subsequently deported because a congressman exposed his history of Nazi activity. And that congressman was a Jew. The man rambled on, in defense of his Nazi colleague. For the rest of the week he tried, but couldn't find anyone who would play bridge with him.

At Jacksonville University, *Geography of a Changing World* was an eye-opener, an innovative approach to what I once considered a boring subject. It turned out to be my all-time favorite course. We delved into location, natural resources, economy, and demographics. We perused maps, prepared graphs, and calculated statistics. Gradually, we were able to determine, for example, why high school drop-out rates in some southern cities were the highest in the country. The handsome young professor confided that our Elderhostel class was his first, and compared our savvy group with his youthful students. "I love teaching seniors," he proclaimed. The only Jewish entity I found in Jacksonville was my cousin Cynthia.

The teachers and personnel I encountered wherever I went have been gracious and helpful. I congratulated the director of one Elderhostel, conducting a markedly efficient program without the usual assistance of a coordinator. "I prefer doing it alone," he confided, "except—when we do a *Jewish Studies* program in the fall. That's when I hire people to assist me. Most of our participants that week are Jewish, and Jews require a lot of attention, you know." *I did know.* Allan King, the comedian, said it all when he quoted a Jewish woman on vacation in the Catskills, complaining to the hotel manager. "The food is terrible, pure poison, inedible—and the portions are so small." I agreed with the director, but if he wasn't a Jew, I might have been offended.

Most Elderhostel accommodations have been upgraded through the years, eligibility age has been reduced to fifty-five, and many programs with specific Jewish content have proliferated. In Maryland, we attended Peabody Institute's Leonard Bernstein marathon, enjoying his famous *Kaddish Symphony* replete with Jewish tradition. His many compositions were inspired by Jewish ritual music and Jewish themes. At Baltimore Hebrew University we toured Jewish historical sights, studied Jewish art, and scrutinized the women in the

Bible. Towsen University's course on Jewish humor elicited non-stop laughter from everyone, Jewish or not.

These days, Arthur and I spend many weeks each summer in the Catskills at one of the largest Jewish Studies Elderhostels in the country. In 1998, they offered me a "one-time" position as a substitute coordinator. I volunteered Arthur as my assistant, and we've been coordinating ever since—checking audio-visual equipment, organizing graduation celebrations, and urging the chef to serve pickled herring and stewed prunes. How lucky can you get?

30

Fortieth Anniversary

Allemande left and *do-si-do. You've got a new partner and what do you know?*

In the summer of 1983, friends invited Arthur and me to join them for an evening of square dancing for beginners, known as "Pedestrians" in square dance lingo. The beat of the singing calls reverberated in my head forever after. So when a beginner's course started up the following year, just two months after I retired, there we were, in our new dancing shoes and matching shirts. Twice a week for four years, we ducked, sashayed, swung, twirled, and promenaded our partners, progressing from Pedestrian to Mainstream to Plus and to Advanced level dancing. Finally, we were ready for the big event, the annual square dance convention in Montreal.

Our fortieth wedding anniversary coincided with the last day of the convention. What a great way to celebrate that milestone occasion. Our children cheered us on, having always enjoyed seeing "cute" photographs of their parents in crinolines and bolo ties. Our younger son's girlfriend, a native of Montreal from an Orthodox Jewish family, arranged for her kid brother to give us a tour of the city. He'd meet us in the lobby of our hotel at three o'clock on Sunday.

For three days Arthur and I *peeled* and *flutterwheeled* with new partners and new callers. What a fun time. We took lots of "cute" pictures and vowed to return the following year. When the convention ended on Sunday afternoon, the date of our Big Four-O, we descended to the lobby of the Queen Elizabeth hotel in search of Kid Brother. Without a red rose or any other identifying object, we found him in that crush of people—a smiling Robert Redford look-alike with a gorgeous blonde on his arm.

"I made reservations at Montreal's best Chinese restaurant, and then we'll tour the city," Redford announced after initial introductions. I suggested doing the tour first, during the daylight hours, but he overruled me, so off we went to "Montreal's best."

At the restaurant we were directed to a rectangular table in a corner of the large dimly lit dining room. Like the Jewish woman in a Jackie Mason comedy routine, I asked for a round table. The maitre d' shook his head and told me that they were all reserved. Overruled once again, I followed him to our designated table, adjacent to a giggling couple who were holding hands and gazing into one another's eyes.

For a short while, as we sipped on jasmine tea and perused the menu, Kid Brother gave us an update on the politics of Montreal. "Corporations are moving out and the best remaining jobs go to the French," he informed us. "It's difficult for young Jews to find work." I was surprised to learn how many of them were leaving the city, known as a mecca for Jews, and moving to places like Toronto, Vancouver, and the United States.

As we talked, I couldn't keep from spying on the loving couple at my elbow. SHE looked like a page out of a '50s magazine, with black harlequin glasses and a pillbox hat atop a blonde Veronica Lake hairdo. HE, with a shaggy red beard, in a khaki soldier's uniform, army cap, and dark glasses, reminded me of Fidel Castro. They appeared to be oblivious of our presence, yet suddenly Veronica glanced over at us.

"Don't I know you?" she asked Redford, whereupon they began an animated conversation in French. Then, smiling broadly, she looked directly at Arthur and me.

"Happy Anniversary," she cooed softly.

"Thank you," we replied in unison. Fidel echoed her greeting.

"Thank you," we answered again, looking directly at him. *Why were these strangers greeting us?*

Slowly it hit me. *His eyes. Her smile.*

"I don't believe it, I don't believe it," I kept repeating, as the tears rolled down my face. Jumping up, we all hugged, kissed, laughed, and cried.

"Didn't you recognize me?" Fidel asked. "I never thought we'd pull this off. I was certain you'd know me in any disguise." He sounded hurt. I too couldn't believe that I had not recognized this man, at whose *brith* I winced, at whose Bar Mitzvah I wept, the child I gave birth to thirty-three years earlier. My son and his girlfriend had fooled both his parents.

"The red beard?" I gasped.

"Dyed."

"The uniform, the blonde wig?"

"Rented."

"When did you get here?"

"We flew in yesterday."

The diners around us, sharing in our surprise, applauded as we continued to embrace, to voice our joy and our disbelief. Fifteen years earlier, I had seen through a twenty-fifth anniversary cover-up, had pretended to be surprised. No one could fool me, I thought. Now my son, playful and imaginative, had orchestrated a surprise that even I could not penetrate.

Redford, hugging his sister, winked at me. "Sorry about the daytime tour," he whispered. I never found out what he did for a living or how he was affected by the Jewish exodus from Montreal.

"I can get you a round table now," the waiter offered.

After dinner the six of us drove up to a hilltop overlooking the city, ablaze in megawatts of electricity and the glow of nighttime moonlight—a magical topping to our most wonderful celebration ever.

31

The Tools Of Her Profession

A senior residence for German Holocaust survivors was under construction in Bayside, just four short blocks from my house. Despite Pa's protestation and Ma's ambivalence, I sent in an application for them. When only a handful of survivors responded, my parents jumped to the top of the list. In 1981, Sam and Clara, both in their eighties, moved out of their apartment in Rego Park and became my neighbors.

In the past, Favorite-Son-in-Law and I drove to see them once a week, but now I stopped by every day, after work, delivering groceries or just to chat. Ma was thrilled. She always had kasha varnishkes and a prize-winning compote concoction on hand for a *nosh*. I accompanied her to a Bingo game and an adventure film in the recreation room. "*Piste zachen*" (empty things), she declared, and never returned. She had more important things to do.

Ma's *nextdorikeh*, Rose, turned out to be a *landsman* from the Old Country. The two of them teamed up with Lily and Molly and became an inseparable foursome. They exchanged recipes, did chair exercises, and attended lectures on health, nutrition, and local politics. Pa and his "guys" were busy too. Holding up their canes to stop traffic, they crossed the street to a small Orthodox synagogue, where they formed the nucleus of a daily *minyan*. Clara and Sam reminded me of youngsters at camp. They dubbed their new home their "Florida Condominium."

Pa died a year later, and Ma carried on alone for over a decade, cooking her favorite Jewish dishes and sharing them with her buddies. Sometimes she even joined them for lunch in the communal dining room, although she claimed the food never had any *tóm* (taste).

When I broke the news that I was planning to retire, I expected my mother to be happy for me.

"You won't be a teacher any more?" she asked incredulously, holding her hands to her head. "What will you do all day? You'll become a *luftmentsh*, a loafer."

"I won't, don't worry. I'll be taking a course in behavioral psychology, a sensory writing workshop, and square dance lessons." I thought I had impressed her.

"*Piste zachen*," she scoffed.

Clara was ninety-three years old when she began to show signs of senile dementia, and for the next six years she needed healthcare aides to assist her. A professional homemaker, she took her job as a housewife seriously; there were so many housewifely things to do. How she resented those aides. They were doing her job, and doing it poorly. "Now," she proclaimed, "I'm a *luftmentsh,* doing *piste zachen.*"

She never found an aide to suit her. They were either sloppy, or noisy, or lazy. Worse yet, the meals they prepared were even less palatable than those she ate in the dining room. Seven days a week they brought her to the lobby where she endured the oft-repeated stories of her neighbors. Rose and Molly were no longer around, and Lilly didn't come down too often. Lobby-sitting was something Ma had little patience for. My sons were rooting for Grandma to make it to her one hundredth birthday, but she died eleven months earlier.

When Favorite-Son-in-Law and I came to clean out her apartment, her presence was everywhere. How could I do this? Looking for mementos to treasure, I found none. She had already given me her entire cache of jewelry: a monogrammed pendant, a friendship ring, and a filigree wedding band. Her one-bedroom apartment had been her castle. Yet this was not the home she had reigned over before the onset of dementia. Her carved mahogany couch, which had remained showcase-new for more than sixty years, was now sagging. The English dresser and night table were discolored and peeling. Searching in her royal domain, the kitchen, I found cracked wedding dishes and chipped enamel pots with broken handles. Had Clara noticed?

As we sorted bits and pieces into rummage containers, Ma was disappearing. Was there nothing to salvage, nothing I could look at or touch that would evoke her memory?

Almost finished sorting and packing, I spotted a crushed, square cardboard carton under a pile of supermarket shopping bags in the hallway closet. Pulling down the band-aid taped box, I lifted out an assortment of wooden mixing spoons, a whisk, and a worn rolling pin. What were Ma's baking utensils doing in this carton?

Visions of my mother preparing a tub of cookie dough or beating egg whites for a sponge cake batter flashed before me. As a young child, I helped her cut out heart-shaped globs that turned into melt-in-your-mouth butter cookies. Food was Clara's way of giving love, and she dispensed lots of it. Our small apartment was always crowded with relatives and friends who dropped in to visit and to sample her cheese blintzes, honey cake, and apple strudel. I like to cook, but I've never baked. Ma provided me with all the cake and cookies I wanted.

Clara refused to accept both my discarded food processor (when I acquired an upgraded model) and the blender I bought for her one Mother's Day. All her grating and shredding and mixing were done by hand. She enjoyed preparing her traditional Jewish recipes for the grandchildren, and years later, on college breaks, they headed straight for her kitchen.

Digging deeper into the carton, I found a variety of worn wood-handled spatulas, two metal hand choppers, and three slotted silver-plated serving spoons that had graced Ma's table at Thanksgiving dinners and Passover *seders*. When had she tucked away these tools of her profession? And why?

Towards the end, Clara couldn't remember what she ate five minutes ago, but she remembered those days long ago, when her home resounded with the hum of family and her kitchen was everybody's favorite restaurant. Ultimately there was just Favorite-Son-in-Law and me. That was all.

"Where's my family?" she asked, over and over again. Even though her grandchildren came to see her, she didn't recall their visits. Only the past—and the two of us—stayed with her. Her dementia progressed steadily, yet strangely, she was always aware of her condition. Had Ma also known what was happening in her apartment? Indeed she had!

Faced with a passing parade of healthcare aides and a deteriorating and disappearing household inventory, Clara figured out a way to preserve her identity. That cardboard carton was her legacy to me.

Although I may never get around to the rolling pin, I putter about in the kitchen wielding Ma's red-handled chopper to decimate an onion, her rounded spatula to flip a batch of salmon latkes, her soup ladle to dole out some split pea soup—and she is with me. My hands on a worn wooden or metal handle—her hands. Cut in more dill, lower the heat, simmer a little longer—her voice.

32

Back To The Catskills - With Elderhostel

Back to the Catskills, the vacation spot of my youth, where Ma took the family for the healing *luft* (air) of "The Mountains." It started with a phone call from Sullivan County Community College Elderhostel (SCCC) in Loch Sheldrake, primarily known for its Jewish Studies curriculum. Would I come up and teach a writing workshop in their summer program?

The marriage of Elderhostel, Jewish Studies, and the Catskills—the combination was intoxicating. My brain went into overload. *I've taken writing workshops and I've published personal essays, but I've never conducted a writing workshop, I've never taught adults, I've never been able to speak before a large* *group. I've never, I've never.* My answer was a reluctant but definitive "No."

Back to the Catskills—working with Elderhostel—the concept percolated in my head. A month later, I accepted an on-site coordinator's position which seemed less threatening than conducting a workshop. I volunteered Arthur as my assistant, and we've been working there ever since. It has been the best of times.

A major perk of my job is getting to sit in on all classes. SCCC Elderhostel offers a variety of intriguing secular courses: History of the Catskills, Musical Theatre and Comedy, Fabulous Fakes in Film, The Secret to Happiness, Social Evolution, Globalization. My favorite subjects are history and world affairs.

Courses in the Jewish Studies program speak to me on another level. I've enjoyed so many of them: Five Jewish Artists, Seven Jewish Justices, History of Jews in America, Conflicting Jewish Viewpoints on Zionism, Judaism and Christianity, Chutzpah, Jewish Film Festival, Jewish Life as Reflected in Literature, Jewish Humor. I've learned a lot, laughed a lot, and rejoiced in my Jewish heritage. I'm delighted when non-Jews, including Nuns, sign up for these programs.

Back to the Catskills, which once boasted over 500 hotels. A handful of them were still operating in 1998, when Arthur and I began working for SCCC. Our Elderhostel programs were held in these remaining grand old mountain resorts, where many surprises awaited me. On my very first assignment, in Greenfield Park, the housekeeping staff went out on strike, and office personnel were making beds and bundling trash. Some rooms were not completed until midnight. Fortunately, dinner, a traditional Catskill feast—from gefilte fish and brisket to strudel—was a culinary triumph, which helped buffer the complaints at Orientation that evening.

In a refurbished hotel in Parksville, a fire broke out at three AM. In varying states of undress, Elderhostelers stood in the chilly October air watching the hotel burn down. We were evacuated to a local high school, where Red Cross volunteers brought us toothbrushes, socks, sweat clothes, and food, while we waited for our director to find a hotel large enough to accommodate us all.

In another resort hotel, featuring an impressive art collection in its lobby, some very religious guests insisted on draping white sheets over the nude sculptures. Our Elderhostelers got a good laugh out of that. By the year 2000 only two viable hotels were still functioning. We eventually settled into The Nevele, in Ellenville, hoping the marriage would survive. It didn't.

"So, what does a coordinator do?" people ask. If they give me an hour or so, I tell them. The major Elderhostel decisions are made by the director, a full-time employee of the college. She is the one who selects the courses, hires the instructors, makes hotel arrangements, and works out the schedule. What's left for me to do? I tell people I'm the "housemother," but Arthur doesn't like that terminology.

"It's incomplete, incorrect, even demeaning," he says. He prefers "facilitator."

Coordinators arrive at the hotel just hours before participants are due to check in. We inspect the conference rooms to see that they are properly set up, and that the audio-visual equipment and air-conditioning are in working order. We set up registration tables, examine the medical forms for special needs, make note of birthdays and anniversaries we will be acknowledging during the week. *Back to the Catskills*, where I am so busy "facilitating," I barely get to breathe the renowned Catskill *luft*.

Elderhostelers line up to pick up their folders and name tags. Who are they? Where do they come from? What do they do? By the end of the week we are not only friends, we become a family, exchanging e-mail addresses and planning get-togethers. My address book is filled with listings of new friends from all over the country. There's Ruthie the librarian from New Jersey, Phyllis and Dan the newlyweds from Westchester, Gilda the party planner from San Diego. When Gilda and I discovered that we were born on the same day, we spent hours uncovering similarities in our lives— Gilda, my "twin." What a loving reunion we had when she returned to SCCC one year.

On the first night we hold an after-dinner orientation session. Lucky thing nobody told me I'd be addressing a group of fifty strangers. I might have turned down the job. In all my years at school, I never volunteered an answer or voiced an opinion. In college, I took as many large lecture courses as possible, so I could get lost in the crowd. It wasn't that I had nothing to say, but that I was too self-conscious to say it. When I contemplated raising my hand, my heart pounded and my face turned red. And here I am, about to conduct a ninety-minute forum.

I force myself to speak by reading from a detailed outline, clarifying the schedule, urging students to locate fire exits, reminding people to rotate seats in the dining room, introducing the instructors, and answering questions. Then, on to the best part of Orientation—personal introductions:

I'm Debra Kerr, whirling round and round—*getting to know you, getting to know all about you.* Some people are reluctant to speak; others would reveal their life histories. I suggest limiting their topics to occupation and major retirement activities. "Elderhostelers do not like hearing about grandchildren," I warn. People nod in agreement and laugh. One woman interpreted my statement as a restriction for the entire week—"Ruth, the grandma bigot."

"I was a bookie," says Sam. "My favorite retirement activity is going to the race track."

"I'm Sybil. I live with Sam. Heidi Fleiss was my boss," says his wife. "I retired when she went to jail." We laugh again—another good group.

Former teachers comprise the largest number of Elderhostelers; you can't keep us out of the classroom. We've got engineers, accountants, social workers, psychologists, salesmen, realtors, librarians, lawyers, businessmen, domestic engineers. One man tells us he's a pediatrician. Later in the week we learn he's not. "With this group, you think I'd admit I'm a cardiologist?" he declares when confronted.

Retirement activities revealed by our Elderhostelers highlight their ingenuity and diversity: recording for the blind, teaching reading to illiterate adults, editing a community newsletter, mediating civil disputes, sculpting, painting, keeping fit, sleeping late. They're political junkies, docents, Little League coaches, published writers, and poets. They sing, they act, they play musical instruments, and they perform as clowns—in nursing homes and children's hospitals. One couple prepares dinner for thirty-five homeless teenagers twice a month. Remarkable! I can hardly wait to "connect" with each of them during the week.

Back to the Catskills, where fielding complaints is a key component of the job. For participants with history in the area, hotel amenities can be disappointing. Memory invokes an image of a grander, more charming, more elegant facility. The hotels we've used are old, and even when renovations total many millions of dollars, Elderhostelers may come upon a leaky ceiling or occasional lack of hot water. The elevator may be out of order and the pool under repair. Fifty seniors? Fifty internal thermostats. It's either "too cold" or "too hot." My main classroom activity becomes that of "thermostat monitor." "Wear layers," I repeat, while nudging Convention Services to adjust the temperature.

Those without history in the area, from California to Texas to Maine, are impressed with the vast acreage, indoor and outdoor pools, golf course, tennis courts, fitness center, and nightclub—featuring live entertainment each evening. Newcomers consider the food wonderful, generous, orgiastic, perhaps.

Catskill alumni recall the vast amounts of it—ethnic and kosher. Because it specializes in Jewish Studies, SCCC Elderhostel has, until recently, offered kosher food. Some Elderhostelers demanded it, most tolerated it, a few grumbled about it. Orgiastic and *kashruth*, however, are no more.

Breakfasts are still expansive: cereal, eggs, bagels, French toast, pancakes, waffles. And, not to worry—stewed prunes. Sometimes there's herring or lox; sometimes bacon and sausages. But, "Where's the pickled salmon and the basket of onion rolls and breakfast cakes?" we ask, with our plates overflowing. The lunch menu may still offer some ethnic treats—potato latkes or blintzes. "They don't taste like they used to," however. There are now three choices for dinner; we remember a dozen. "Compare our food to other Elderhostels, not to the old Catskills," I implore. The famous "Borscht Belt" has gradually disappeared.

Back to the Catskills with Elderhostel, where I experience a personal growth spurt each time I go up. But it is not the Catskill *luft* that is the catalyst. The unspoken perks of the job are many—intangible and major.

Coordinators become audio-visual technicians, health consultants, psychotherapists, teachers, crisis managers.

Arthur produces an end-term celebration event and serves as its master of ceremonies. He gives a brief lecture on the history of the Catskills, once the country's largest resort area, and discusses the prospects for its future. I have learned to address a large group without panicking, and I follow his talk with activity suggestions for our one unscheduled afternoon. A microphone enhances my voice and empowers me. Practice does indeed make perfect.

"Would you be interested in an after-class writing workshop?" I asked my group one day. They were, and we did. The output from the Elderhostelers, some of whom had never written before, was creative and insightful. They wanted more. So I did it again, and yet again. I was comfortable with it, and triumphant.

Like a Boy Scout, a coordinator's motto is "Be Prepared." I've yet to help an Elderhosteler cross the road, but I paired a lonely freshman with an upbeat veteran, and the two women laughed together happily all week. "My room is cold," Eric told me. "Turn off your air conditioner," I quipped. And he did. George was frantically searching the hotel for his "missing wife," and I found her—in their room. I couldn't help Lillian, who called at midnight, complaining about a fly that was keeping her awake. Subsequently, I purchased a fly swatter.

From the time she was a young girl, until well into her nineties, my Yiddishe Mama was busy "helping out"—her parents, her sister, her sister-in-law, her cousins, her neighbors, her daughter. She cooked, she baked, she scrubbed, she shlepped, she baby-sat. I did not follow in her footsteps.

But here I am—*Back to the Catskills* with Elderhostel—and that's my job, "helping out." It feels so good. Ma would be *kvelling*.

33

The Big Divide

Nine-Eleven brought Americans together. The Big Divide began when Congress voted to give the president power to initiate military action against Iraq if necessary.

"We've got to teach the Iraqis a lesson and prevent another terrorist attack," my cousin shouted over the phone.

"There's no connection between the terrorists and Iraq. Bush came into office intending to invade Iraq. Nine-Eleven gave him the excuse he needed," I responded, matching her voice in tempo and pitch. I hung up trembling. My cousin was my lifelong friend; we'd never before raised our voices in anger at one another.

After the United States launched the war in Iraq, the divide intensified. It appeared to me that people were looking at one another furtively, their eyes asking the unspoken question: *Are you for or against the war?*

My hairdresser trimmed my curly locks and whispered, "Some of the girls in the shop are barely talking to each other; my best friend accused me of being unpatriotic." My dentist probed my wisdom tooth, and confided that his office staff was divided. So was the block he lived on; neighbors were glaring at one another. Confrontations with friends, colleagues, and relatives were loud and heated.

Worst of all was the tension created within the Jewish community. Israel became the main issue, some claiming "the war was good for Israel," others insisting "it would increase terrorism and make it worse."

The presidential campaign of 2004, highlighting the issues of the economy, religion, the ground war, and mounting casualties further accelerated the debate and underscored the division among us. The GOP wooed Jewish Democrats and emotions were strong. An article in the *Jewish Week* quoted Floridian voters:

"I'm voting Republican, and people tell me they can't believe I'm Jewish. My main concerns are Israel and terrorism."

"I'm voting for Bush because he's one of the best presidents in support of Israel."

I wanted to tell them that I'm an American, and I vote in the best interests of my own country.

This time around, the dialogue went underground, partisan e-mails flying back and forth, but only to like-minded folk, to like-minded Jews.

"Consider the following quotation and cast your ballot as you see fit," my cousin Judy wrote.

"Naturally, the common people don't want war, but after all, it is the leader of a country who determines the policy, and it is always a simple matter to drag people along whether it is a democracy or a fascist dictatorship . . . All you have to do is to tell them they are being attacked, and denounce the pacifist for lack of patriotism and exposing the country to danger. It works the same in every country."

Herman Goering at the Nuremberg trials (4.18.46)

I never imagined I'd be in agreement with the infamous Herr Goering.

The overwhelming majority of my friends and relatives joined me in the anti-war camp. Team members without uniform, we identified our opponents and avoided political commentary when we were with them. For a short while titillating remarks heard at the Academy Awards became my favorite subject for discussion, but in the end even that proved to be provocative. The antagonism between pro-war and anti-war Jews was not like the playful bantering between *Galitzianers* and *Litvaks*. Ultimately, we just avoided one another.

After the election, civil war in Iraq escalated, the casualty count grew, and the president's approval rating dropped into the basement. Some of my pro-war acquaintances abandoned support for administration policies, and they too began forwarding partisan e-mails, venting their frustration. "This war has made us less secure," wrote a former Bush supporter from California. Presidential advisors departed the government. Others were fired.

Increasingly, pundits devised exit strategies, declaring the war had empowered Iran and increased terrorism in the Middle East. "Getting out will mean disaster for Israel," bemoaned an old friend during dinner one evening, revealing his political position for the first time. "Everyone I know agrees with you," he added, "but the president is doing the right thing."

A social gathering we both attended turned into a Bush-bashing party. "Bush is a *shlemiel*," a guest proclaimed. Everyone grunted in approval.

"He's a *shlemazel*," my old friend quickly replied. No one except me knew that he agreed with the president and they all missed his meaning. "Yeah, yeah," they agreed loudly, "he's a *shlemazel*."

Definition: A *shlemiel* is one who spills soup on the *shlemazel*. "Poor Bush, he gets dumped on," is what my friend really meant.

The anger smolders, the schism remains, the chasm among friends and relatives widens. How do we handle holidays and family dinners? My son, a talk-show host, recommends "holding your political tongue." A caller proclaims he is making "a clean break" with his sister and brother. "Find a fun distraction, like a group game," says another. Only one caller suggests "fighting the good fight." Everyone agrees we've got a big problem.

My cousin and I exchange e-mails occasionally and see each other at major family events.

"Hello, how are you?"

"I'm fine, how are you?" We hugged long and hard when we bumped into each other in a theatre lobby, then both of us ran off in different directions. Not included in the official casualty count, invisible but very real, are the interpersonal relationships of all Americans, and American Jews in particular, that have been irrevocably scarred.

34

Peace, When?

In 1948, just three months after the State of Israel was born, I graduated from college, married my high school sweetheart, embarked on my teaching career, and signed up for graduate courses. Four years later I became a stay-at-home mom immersed in the life-altering experience of raising two funny frisky sons. When my younger son entered kindergarten, I went back to the classroom. Arthur and I bought a house, and I found a second career—furnishing it. My weekends were spent foraging through flea markets and antique fairs, negotiating with vendors for old tables, rockers, clocks, and trunks. During that busy happy time I was only subliminally aware of the ongoing hostility between the Jewish State and its Arab neighbors.

When I was a teenager, I learned about the expulsion of Jews from Spain in 1492. At the same time, I learned that the relationship between Muslims and Jews in that country had been amicable. Rabbi Sherwin Wine, founder of the Society of Humanistic Judaism, affirms that "for most of the past 1400 years . . . there was a compatibility of spirit and practice between the Jewish and Muslim societies that did not exist between the Jews and the Greco-Roman culture of the Christian world."

In the late nineteenth and early twentieth centuries, Zionists sought to escape the ongoing slaughter and demonization of Jews in Christian Europe by establishing a Jewish nation in the biblical land of Israel, within the Muslim world. "While the Jews saw themselves as the victims of Christian anti-Semitism," Wine wrote, "the Muslims saw the Zionists as the last invasion of European colonists." Arabs and Muslims perceived this as "a travesty of justice," and it triggered "hatred of the Jews that had not existed before."**

The way I understand it, a coalition of Arab nations pledged to destroy the new country even before it was declared a state in 1948. Economic boycott, border wars, arms build-up—I hadn't heard much about them. In 1967, when Egypt expelled the United Nation's peacekeepers from the Sinai Peninsula, proclaimed a blockade of the Israeli port of Eilat, and called for unified Arab action against Israel, I woke up to what was happening outside the picket fence of my life in the U.S.A.

Fearing an imminent invasion, Israel launched a preemptive attack against Egypt's air force. The "Six-Day War" was fought between Israel and its neighbors. At the end of the war, Israel had gained control of the Gaza Strip, the

West Bank, eastern Jerusalem, and the Golan Heights. The Israeli victory was humiliating. Rabbi Wine notes that the Arab world blamed their defeat on a giant world Jewish conspiracy, and "turned hatred into anti-Semitism."

Shortly after the war, I heard Abba Eban, Israel's Foreign Minister and former Ambassador to the United States, speak to a packed house at Colden Auditorium in Queens College and warn of the consequences of occupying land with a million Arabs on it. How right he was. The establishment of settlements, and their subsequent expansion, exacerbated the hostility in the region and promoted world-wide hostility toward Israel and the Jews.

The Arabs, on the other hand, were committed to the destruction of Israel before those settlements were ever built. What is the probability for peace, with or without settlements, as long as Israel's right to exist continues to be rejected?

In 1976, Arthur and I took an eighteen day trip to Israel. After a week of touring the outwardly thriving and peaceful country, our guide brought us to the Arab market in Jerusalem, admonishing our group to return to the bus in one hour. One hour for the much touted Arab market? I was an antique collector, a flea market enthusiast. One hour was barely enough time for even a quick overview. The huge display of crafts and antiquities was dazzling. Weaving through the throng of shoppers, I fancied a bronze jewelry box here, a carved mahogany tray there. Vendors approached me eagerly and were more than anxious to negotiate, to make a deal. My adrenalin was pumping, and I resolved to return during free time.

Alas, when Arthur and I did so a few days later, the Arab market was shut down. Not a seller, a buyer, a jewelry box, or tray in sight. Police with clubs and guns, grim and silent, cordoned off the area. The Tower of David, adjacent to the market, seemed deserted and unguarded, so we sneaked inside and climbed to the top. It was eerie up there, looking down on the swarm of police and the vast empty grounds which had been teeming with people and activity only a few days earlier.

Until that morning, I had toured Israel like I'd done in England or in Italy—delving into its history, its art and architecture. Walking along the streets of Tel Aviv, peering into faces that looked like my family, and speaking Yiddish to local shopkeepers, had added another, richer dimension. Suddenly the truth hit me—I was in a war zone! Our tour guide wouldn't talk about the incident that had precipitated the police action; bad for business, I imagine. Unable to return to the market when it reopened, my visit ended without another opportunity to negotiate.

While in Israel, we spent some time with old friends, a couple who had made *Aliyah* (become Israeli citizens) in the late sixties. They had befriended some of their Arab neighbors, most especially one woman, who had become a close friend. I was pleased to learn that some fraternization between Arab and Jew was taking place. Years later, on a visit to the United States, this Israeli couple informed us that during the first *Intifada* (Palestinian uprising) in 1988, their good friend and all the other Arabs they knew had mysteriously disappeared! Having learned that the Intifada included intra-Palestinian violence and the execution of approximately 1100 alleged Palestinian "collaborators," I don't think their disappearance is such a mystery. Those Israeli Arabs, fearing for their lives should they be seen "collaborating" with their Jewish friends, chose to live.

Twenty years later, the hostility persists—suicide bombers, rockets, missiles, terrorist attacks, border closings, retributions, assassinations, checkpoint harassments, failed peace summits—horrendous, crazy-making. As an elementary school teacher, mother, and grandmother, what disturbs me most about the Middle East conflict are the children, growing up under the umbrella of fear and hate, in a military culture, thinking that war is normal.

Palestinian and settler children throw rocks at one another. Israeli school girls write messages on bombs that are used to kill. I have read vile and ugly expressions of hate from both Jewish and Muslim youngsters. I've not seen evidence that anti-Arab bigotry is promulgated in Israeli schools, but children in mosques and Islamic schools are taught that Jews are the sons of monkeys and pigs, and that killing them is a holy deed. Rodgers and Hammerstein said it: *You've Got To Be Carefully Taught*. How can hate translate into peace?

217

Anti-Israel and anti-Jewish incidents soar all over the globe—fallout from the Middle East conflict. Israel has become "the Jew," and "the Jew," Israel. History tells me that Jew hatred will never disappear. Israel is but an excuse for endemic anti-Semitism.

While the acceptance of Jews into a non-Jewish United States of America is historically unparalleled, anti-Semitism is once again visible here too. Methodist, Lutheran, and Presbyterian groups, along with the Green Party and City Council groups propose economic boycotts and anti-Israel divestment resolutions. We see anti-Israel movements on our campuses. Holocaust deniers seem to pop up everywhere. It's not uncommon to hear "Jews run the media," "Jews control the banks," "Jews killed Jesus." Conservative commentator Ann Coulter remarks that Jews need to be "perfected" by converting to Christianity. Ann, do I have a reading assignment for you!*

The United Nations has been more than a disappointment to me; it has broken my heart. Too often it has failed in its primary mission—keeping the peace. It ignores genocide, supports totalitarian regimes, and escalates its record of anti-Semitism. I added my name to World Jewish Congress and Weisenthal Center petitions urging the UN to take a stand against violence and anti-Semitism. Eleanor Roosevelt—chairperson of the Commission on Human Rights and world traveler calling for nuclear disarmament—we need you!

Doing nothing makes me want to scream. My sons are products of the activist Sixties. They both joined Vietnam

War protesters speaking out "against the insanity of war." My younger son recalls the "Moratorium," a national "strike," which took place in cities all over the country: "That was October 15, 1969, so I was all of fourteen years old, and had very little understanding of why we were in Vietnam, but not being in that war, or in any war, made perfect sense to me." In 2004, he contributed his artistry to the design of a peace banner, thousands of which were displayed at the Republican National Convention. My older son, a radio and television talk-show host, devotes himself to searching for common ground with his diverse listeners. There's a preponderance of hate and divisive voices in the media these days, and I'm heartened by the response to his kind of journalism that "builds community rather than divides it."

More than forty years ago, I began writing letters of protest and support—to politicians, presidents, jurists, and journalists. I'm grateful for the computer which has made the process so much easier for me. How much of my impassioned correspondence has been read? I wonder. Men seem to be better at responding. Russell Baker sent a long handwritten reply. A First Lady, a prominent television personality, and a Supreme Court Justice never answered.

At Elderhostel, I met an outspoken ninety-year-old, a member of the Seattle "Raging Grannies," an anti-war protest group with affiliates around the country, Canada, and elsewhere in the world. Peace poetry was her game. She wrote. She sang. But did she conquer? A raging grandma myself, the idea of Granny Power possessed me. I could not shake it. I imagined a worldwide outpouring of gray-haired grandmas converging on their presidents, prime ministers, premiers, grand viziers, kings, queens, and warlords. Grandmother is a powerful word. The leaders beat their weapons into plowshares and restored peace on earth. *Peace, When? Peace, Then!* Waking up to reality, I tried, but could not find a "Raging Grannies" group anywhere in the New York area.

In 2007, an Ahmadiyya mosque replaced a Reform synagogue in my borough of Queens. I was unaware of its orientation until the spring of 2009 when the new religion on the block invited a broad spectrum of spiritual leaders and their members to a peace conference. Fifteen speakers reiterated the message of honoring and respecting one another as the key to achieving peace, love, and harmony in a diverse society. I was moved by the unexpected buffet served at the conclusion of the event, most significantly its kosher table: roast chicken, Israeli salad, and vegetarian *cholent*. The message of outreach to the community was evident. The larger issue of the Israeli-Palestinian conflict, however, was not addressed. I would have liked some interchange of ideas on that subject.

Peace talks have not had a good track record in the Middle East. Hostilities will end only when both sides overrule the zealots and affirm their desire and priority for true peace. Nevertheless, I rejoice when I hear that Israel and Syria are "talking," that a cease fire agreement has been reached, or that a peace conference is in the works. As a flea market romantic, I know the value of negotiation. Like

South Pacific's **Nurse Nellie,** *I'm a cockeyed optimist, stuck like a dope on a thing called hope.* Maybe this time . . .

*READING ASSIGNMENT FOR ANN COULTER

In 1989, speaking before the Foundation for Christian Rescuers, a project of the ADL, John Cardinal O'Connor declared that "Centuries of Christian persecution of the Jews laid the groundwork for Nazi genocide. Essentially it was my people—my people," he said, "who brought about the Holocaust. I share the anguish and the agony of what happened to the Jews. You Jews—never permit yourselves or your children to forget the suffering. You Christians—never forget the guilt."

In 2000, Pope John Paul II embarked on a pilgrimage to Israel, where he prayed at the Western Wall, then composed a note on a small piece of paper and thrust it between the wall's cracks. "We are deeply saddened," he wrote, "by the behavior of those who in the course of history have caused these children of yours to suffer, and asking your forgiveness. We wish to commit ourselves to genuine brotherhood with the people of the Covenant." Yad Vashem, Israel's Holocaust museum, retrieved the note, and it was exhibited at New York's Museum of Jewish Heritage in 2006 for everyone to read.

** Sherwin Wine. "Jews and the Muslim World," The Humanistic Shofar, Queens Community for Cultural Judaism, December, 2008.

35

Hilton Head, South Carolina

The lure of the ocean! It propelled me to Orchard Beach when I was a teenager in the Bronx; to Jones Beach or to Long Beach as an adult; walking on the boardwalk, inhaling the fresh ocean air, delighting in the collision of sky, sand, and water.

When we were both retired, Arthur and I vacationed in coastal areas for a month each winter—Spain, Portugal, Greece, Mexico, the Carolinas, Georgia, and finally, Florida. For five years we returned to Deerfield Beach. In lieu of a boardwalk, we took morning walks on the hard concrete pavement adjacent to the beach. When the temperature-humidity index soared one day, we piled our suitcases into the car and headed home, aiming to make our first overnight stop at Hilton Head, an island resort in South Carolina. I don't like hot. Hot fries my brain and dries up my creative juices. I like mild, breezy, and brisk. And that's what I found at Hilton Head.

Tall palm trees, massive oaks, skinny pines, and lush hanging foliage greeted us as we drove onto the hotel grounds. Almost sundown, we checked in, unloaded our luggage, and headed for the beach, unprepared for the scene that awaited us. There was no boardwalk. We plowed through a short strip of thick soft sand, the kind of sand one would typically find in Jones Beach. And then suddenly, there it was—a huge expanse of firm flat smooth beach extending all the way to the surf. Hundreds of people, walking, jogging, and bicycling on Mother Nature's own treadmill, the perfect surface I'd been seeking all of my adult life.

What started as an overnight stop turned into a permanent winter retreat. It's been eight years now since Arthur and I began renting a condo apartment in Hilton Head, known for its golf and tennis. We don't golf, and Arthur plays more tennis at home than on the island. It's the "walking beach" that beckons, so easy on my back.

Depending on the tide, weather, and time of day, the scene reinvents itself each time we appear. The beach could be a large swatch of beige cloth the size of a football field, a narrow band of packed wet sand no wider than my driveway, or a striated cluster of sandy islands around which I carefully maneuver. The bright sun beams slivers of gold onto the dark blue water, sandwiched between the pale blue sky and the matching stripe of shallow water along the surf. A rumbling ocean deposits clumps of white foam on the beach some days, gently washes over the sand on others—each scene more breathtaking than the next.

On concrete or blacktop, I find anything longer than a thirty-minute walk too tiring. But on this beach I'm able to walk for an hour each morning, in my wide-brimmed sun-hat and SP30 sunscreen, stopping to pluck a few seashells from the sand and to gawk at an egret or a school of dolphins. Before sundown, I return yet again, for my evening *fix*. This beach is my personal piece of heaven.

Between beach walks, Arthur and I shop and put together simple healthy gluten-free meals. We don't go out to dinner much; it's hard to find a vegetable plate or a plain piece of fish on the island. I use my computer for writing and for listening to New York talk-radio. We go to the bridge club or to a movie. We take the forty minute drive to Savannah or nearby Beaufort for a concert, or a day of antiquing and gallery hopping. When it rains I may go to Belk's Department store, or browse through a chic boutique in one of the little shopping malls flanked with palmettos and exotic flowers. The outlet malls in nearby Bluffton are a bargain-hunter's delight. Best of all is attending the week-long International Piano Competition each March. What a treat! For one month I pretend I'm a resident of this resort island.

Occasionally, we attend Friday night services at the local temple, not something we're likely to do at home. The rabbi is a friendly, cherubic Red Sox fan who dislikes the New York Yankees with a passion. I wouldn't want him to come upon Arthur on the beach, wearing his Yankee baseball cap.

There is no official cantor. Congregants provide the music, playing the piano or the guitar, and leading the members in song. Services are brief, much of it in English. The public service announcements reveal the multifaceted social activities of the congregants. Guests are invited to introduce themselves and to join in the *Oneg* which follows. Nibbling on a chocolate-dipped strawberry, I get to meet some of the Jewish residents in this small southern town with thirty-five churches and one synagogue.

We paired up with one couple for Swiss teams at the bridge club. A tennis player we befriended calls Arthur to fill-in with his foursome. Snowbirds from Connecticut invited us for *Shabbat* dinner before going on to services one evening. We reconnected with another temple couple when we linked arms at a square dance. These contacts, however, are casual and infrequent. We spend most of the time by ourselves. I've learned to appreciate the tranquility.

One summer, at our Catskill Elderhostel, we met Kathy and Bernie, newly retired to Hilton Head. Most weeks, when they're not visiting their grandchildren out-of-town, we manage to meet for dinner or a movie. We've called them when looking for a walk-in medical center, when we've needed an auto mechanic, and for advice on the safety of drinking local tap water. They have become our island "family."

We were so pleased when Kathy and Bernie invited us to a Friday night meeting of a *Chaverah* (Jewish friendship group) formed in recent years, especially since we had been considering joining such a group at home. The traditional blessings over the candles, the wine, and the *challah* pre-ceded a splendid potluck *Shabbat* meal. A topic of Jewish interest is discussed at each of these monthly get-togethers. That night, Bernie presented a comprehensive disserta-tion on European Jews in the *shtetl* before World War I. Members shared their personal history—a *haimish* (homey), heartwarming evening. I applaud the group's mission "to gather in fellowship to enhance their Jewish heritage and values while respecting the unique vision of each member, be it religious, spiritual or social." Our return visit this past winter was equally uplifting.

"How do you like living here?" we ask people we meet everywhere—at the bridge club, the piano festival, the temple, the *Chaverah*—people who have retired to Hilton Head.

"Beats New England weather."

"Great golf."

"Fantastic bridge club."

"Heavenly beach." They all agree it was the best deci-sion they'd ever made.

"Why don't you move down?" they want to know. If it were not for my family living in New York City, I might consider it.

A major drawback to living in sunny South Carolina would be its conservative political climate. A new Jewish resident we met, a lifelong Democrat, voted Republican for the first time after he relocated. "When in Rome . . . ," he shrugged. Does that mean if he goes to Rome, he'll become

Catholic? "People don't talk politics around here," he told us. For me that would be close to impossible.

I've witnessed the setting sun time and again throughout the years: dipping between tall buildings, through forests, and below seaside restaurants; in Key West, as I cued up with the tourists on the boardwalk; at Little Neck Bay, where I go for my daily walks at home. But only once, driving north through New Jersey with my family in 1967, had I seen the sun rise—until I came to Hilton Head.

We rented our first ocean-front condo in 2008. I woke up earlier than usual one morning; it seemed like the sky was on fire. Dashing to the window, I saw luminous bands of deep red, pink, and orange striating across huge billowy clouds. As I stood there, mesmerized, the colors faded, the sky resumed its usual blue gray hue, and the sun suddenly appeared. It struck me as a metaphor for my daily life—focusing on the sunset, ignoring the sunrise. I took it as a wake-up call.

The next morning, looking for an encore, I waited for the fiery sky to materialize. Instead, I saw only a faint pink stripe, followed by a small crescent sun peeking out from behind the horizon. Within seconds, the sun emerged in its entirety, in all its blinding glory. Morning after morning the sun changed its entrance, the more clouds there were, the more awesome the sight. Words cannot fully describe the scene. Perhaps an artist can do it justice.

I could hardly wait for a repeat performance when we returned to Hilton Head this past March. Back in Bayside, away from the ocean, I do not get to see the first speck of sun peeking over the horizon, but focus instead on the sunlight flooding my living room most mornings.

36

Community

My mother tried to bribe me. "I'll bring *Shabbes* dinner every week, and fish latkes, and kasha varnishkes. I'll baby-sit on weekends. If you want to go back to work, I'll come every day . . ." The baby was our first-born son, then two months old. We were living in a studio apartment off the Grand Concourse in the Bronx, and a larger apartment in the building had just become available. Ma wanted me to take it.

But I was headed to Queens, a more suburban borough of New York City, away from concrete and six-story apartment buildings, to a brand new garden apartment complex—Clearview Gardens, in Whitestone. It wasn't a private house, which would have been my first preference, but it was the closest thing to it. For me, it was like moving to the country.

In the early 1950s, co-op garden apartments, middle in-
come hi-rise buildings, and small one-family dwellings were
sprouting up throughout the borough. The Baby Boomer
era was upon us. The preponderance of new residents to
our co-op complex, mostly in their twenties, moved in with
an infant in tow, or one on the way. It was not long before
I became part of a new mom's group, which soon became
my major support group. I thought Queens was a predomi-
nantly Gentile borough, but it seemed to me that most of
the newcomers to "Clearview" came from the Bronx or from
Brooklyn—and were Jewish.

It was quite a trip from Ma's apartment in the Bronx to
northeastern Queens: first, a twenty minute hike to West
Farms Road; then, waiting for the Q44 bus to Flushing,
traveling over the Whitestone Bridge, and finally, changing
to the Q16 bus directly to Clearview Gardens. It took her
two hours to get there, shlepping shopping bags full of lin-
ens, and things like woolen slip-overs, Swee-Touch-Nee tea
bags, cheese blintzes, and matzo-ball soup. "It reminds me
of Europe," she said disparagingly, looking around at the
low-rise attached garden apartments. Anything resembling
the Old Country brought back bad memories.

Large grass courtyards dotted with newly planted trees,
and miniature playgrounds secluded behind building clusters, were filled with active toddlers. Our group of young
mothers gathered around the sandbox each day, talking
about diaper service, the price of bananas, or our favorite brisket recipe for the next holiday dinner. If any of the
women attended synagogue, I was unaware of it. Some kept

a kosher kitchen and shopped at a kosher butcher, the only discernable religious observance among us. Raised in immigrant Ashkenazi working families, we favored the New Deal policies that President Roosevelt had instituted. My friends and I joined the local chapter of American Jewish Congress (AJC), a political action organization focusing on social justice and separation of church and state. We emerged as a community with a strong sense of cultural identity and warm interpersonal relationships.

In 1963, after ten years of garden apartment living, Arthur and I realized the American Dream. We bought our own home, a five-year-old Cape Cod in a Bayside development, ten minutes away from our friends in Whitestone. On the day we moved in, one neighbor advised us to change our locks; the angry ex-husband of the former owner could be lurking. Another brought us a strawberry shortcake. Groups of children could be seen playing ball on the streets and in the pocket park at the corner. By the end of the month our sons had each acquired a new best friend, and we had been invited to a festive neighborhood party. A short walk around the block took an hour; there were so many people to talk with. It seemed like almost everyone we met began the conversation with, "Do you play bridge?" We did. Bayside became an extension of the community we'd known in Whitestone.

Our boys, ages seven and ten, were old enough to embark on a Jewish education, which meant joining a synagogue, thereby making a choice for our family's religious affiliation. Our friends in Clearview and in Bayside were doing the same, transforming us into a community of "identified" Jews—Conservative or Reform. None were Orthodox, some remained unaffiliated. My family chose a Reform temple outside the immediate neighborhood, which most closely reflected our leanings, but added a transportation burden to our very busy lives.

I was teaching at a neighborhood elementary school and taking graduate courses in the late afternoon. Arthur was working as an engineer during the day, teaching at a community college and going to graduate school in the evenings. Family members did not live next door, as they did in the Bronx, but many of them lived close enough for frequent get-togethers. In 1981, my parents moved to a senior residence a few blocks away, and I aimed to spend some time with them every day.

I attended Women's American ORT meetings with my Bayside friends, subscribed to Queens Symphony concerts with my teacher friends, and formed new friendships in a ballroom dancing class at a nearby junior high school. On Friday nights Arthur and I played duplicate bridge in Bayside, and on Saturday nights we enjoyed intimate dinner parties with our Clearview crowd. We had all the social activity we could handle, and never became part of the temple community.

The connectedness we had enjoyed began to change in the late 1980s, when our closest friends, the Taylors, bought a house in New Jersey, and the Ginsburgs, our backyard neighbors, moved to a leisure village in Connecticut. In the early 1990s, the makeup of our eight-couple Friday night bridge group was altered when fully half its members re-located to Florida. We ran out of replacements when the Jaffes flew off to San Diego to be near their sons. After thirty years, the game ended. Our next-door neighbor moved to Manhattan, our down-the-block neighbors became realtors in the Catskills, others passed away. Now it only takes me seven minutes to walk around the block.

Our new neighbors reflect what is happening in all of Queens, the most ethnically diverse locality in the United States. Efforts at friendship begin with, and end with, a friendly greeting. "Hi, how are you?" "Happy holiday." "Nice weather." "It looks like rain." Although we had never sought out a Jewish neighborhood, it had empowered us. We were family, much like it had been in the Bronx.

I miss the community I had, the community that has disappeared, but an expanded social structure has evolved over the years. A combined group of women from Clearview, AJC, and Great Neck adult education gather in fellowship for birthday luncheons. My friend Naomi, who moved to Westchester a decade ago, drops by on the way home from her Queens hairdresser for short, but intimate tête-à-têtes. Arthur and I go to a bridge club one afternoon a week, and we await the return of several bridge-playing "snowbirds" each spring. Our bi-weekly Jewish Humanist meetings provide stimulating Saturday afternoons. An out-of-neighborhood book discussion group keeps our reading material current; a writing group keeps me on my toes. We exchange Christmas gifts with our Korean neighbors.

Happy New Year 2009! It's time to reflect and to reevaluate.

Should we sell our house? Get rid of the gardener and the snow removal service? Long ago we ruled out joining our friends frolicking in the southern sun. What about moving to a low maintenance apartment? Or a jumping senior community? In the future, perhaps; but for now, we're staying put. How can I give up the room of my own, nine large closets, a screened-in deck? Where would I put the ping-pong table, our family gathering place for round-robin tournaments?

New York City is where my children and grandchildren live. New York City is where my heart is. I love walking the streets, like a tourist, head angled to the sky, observing the varied architecture—from Battery Park to Washington Heights. People-watching, in this city of eight million, is a sociological adventure. A tolerable drive, and a network of public transportation make it possible for me to choose from a huge variety of enticing cultural events at the 92nd Street Y, the JCC, Lincoln Center, libraries, museums, universities, and synagogues all over the Metropolitan area. Importantly, pulling me like a giant magnet, is that global icon of theatre—Broadway. Greater New York has become my community.

ACKNOWLEDGMENTS

This collection of essays may never have become a book were it not for my husband, Arthur. He tackled the exasperating problems I encountered with the computer and assisted me with research. He took command of the kitchen and of the telephone. He acted as liaison with the publisher, an arduous task. Would you believe, he read the first draft of each of my stories, saw no necessity for further edits, and nodded his approval? Bless him.

Both my sons, Brian and Warren, were always there for me—on the computer, at the other end of the phone line, or at family dinners where I cornered them for a second opinion on a segment I'd written. Warren, author and graphic artist, designed the book cover, book jacket, title pages, and table of contents. He counseled me on typography and helped me with countless editorial decisions.

My brother-in-law Sam Lehrer shared his knowledge and wisdom. Cousins Morris Josepher, Sara Alderman, and Claire Siegel filled in details of our family history. Daughter-in-law Vicki Dennis and my friends Muriel Lilker, Naomi Patlis, and Vivienne Swetow became my quick-fix comma and syntax *mavens*. Friends and family recognized my need for alone time. Mary Kay Blakely, who taught "Writing the Personal Essay" at the New School for Social Research, awakened me to this reflective and compelling genre in 1988. Her encouragement to seek out a writers' group led me to Tuesday night sessions in the diner with Anne Bianco, Hannah Garson, Ted and Roberta Krulik, Muriel Lilker, and Rita Plush.

I thank you all.